ISLAND AT WAR

THE LIGHTHOUSE KIDS

Spirits of Cape Hatteras Island

ISLAND AT WAR

Jeanette Gray Finnegan Jr.

POINT
PUBLISHING

ISBN 978-0-578-46566-1

First Printing

DEDICATION

Jeanette Gray Finnegan

As this is the final book of a five series set on the history of Cape Hatteras island, the set is dedicated to my mother, Jeanette Gray Finnegan (Sr.)

My mother began her journey as a scholar when she was eighteen years old with only one year of college. She came home from East Carolina Teachers College in Greenville, North Carolina, but after the first summer was convinced by locals to teach in one of the villages for a small sum paid by each parent whose child attended. She eventually taught in the villages of Hatteras, Buxton, and Kinnakeet (Avon). She taught the first three grades all in the same room. This she did for several years through World War II.

After the war, my father returned and was assigned to a Naval Base in Norfolk, Virginia. The family moved and she took a job teaching first grade, on the stipulation she enter college and get her degree. This she did during summers and taking night classes. I never remember a time when I was in school that she was not also studying. After obtaining her undergraduate degree, she continued on to get her master's degree in Education at nearby William and Mary College in Williamsburg, Virginia, more than one hour away. She eventually served as the Principal in four elementary schools. She retired as the Assistant Personnel Director of Norfolk City Schools.

Upon retiring, she moved "home" to the village of her birth. It was at her request that I research the history of this island, with the intention of writing these books. She complained that she had become aware that the only books on the subject were written by "strangers". To my mother, a stranger was anyone she did not know had original roots several generations deep. So, if one moves to the island, that was not sufficient to qualify them as a native. That might make one a "local", but to her, unless she knew your parents, grandparents, and so on down the line, you were a "stranger".

It was her wish that I record our life as it was when we were not connected to the mainland. Maybe it was her life she wanted recorded.

She was correct. Doing research on the period from 1598 to the present revealed more than I had ever suspected. She was also surprised, and pleased. She died at age 102, almost blind, and taken care of by nurses. These ladies read my manuscripts to her, one or two chapters each night, like bedtime stories, and she did hear manuscripts one, two and three. She lamented several times that she couldn't wait to hold them in her hands, which never happened.

Mom, here they are. I hope you recognize your wonderful life and contributions.

CONTENTS

Acknowledgments ix

Prologue xi

1. War 1

2. Independence 17

3. War of 1812 31

4. Ellie's Dream: The Sea Fights Back 49

5. The Cave 65

6. Civil War 83

7. Adventure 103

8. Underground Buxton 121

9. World War I 141

10. They Were Valiant 159

11. The War Is Over 179

12. The Day the Dolphin Surfed 193

Epilogue: Interesting Facts about the Island 211

ACKNOWLEDGMENTS

There are always people other than the writer who contribute to the success of a project. These are those people in my professional life.

TED To my loving husband, who has laughed with me, fought with me, read every page at least six times. Memorized all of them, and spouts them out to strangers interested in buying my work. He has more faith in me than I have in myself, and he doesn't hesitate to pick me off the floor when I have talked myself down.

Thank you Ted, you are my hero.

LUZ M. ALVA-BULLOCK Luz walked me through my first publishing experience. She had faith in my work. Nobody had seen the type of things I envisioned for my books, but she did.

We talked often. She even made a trip to the island to become more familiar with everything I was trying to portray.

Thanks Luz. I am forever in your debt.

KATIE SEVERA My dearest Katie, the artist who worked on the covers and layout for the five books. We never met, but I have been corresponding with her since book one. Every time I wrote a new book, I had Katie put the new animals on the cover. We both scoured for pictures of white dolphin, red horse, three horses, red, blue/black, and palomino, a raven and so on. The covers are wonderful.

Exactly what I envisioned.

Thank you, Katie, you are my genius!

PROLOGUE

Cape Hatteras is the vacation destination for over two and a half million people looking for rest, relaxation, exercise, and accommodations. From the ten bedroom mansion to the cozy cottage on the water, delicious food from local seafood, shops filled with the finest art, open air concerts on the beach, or simply smores over an open campfire next to the ocean, all are draws to this quiet island.

Welcoming all is the Cape Hatteras Lighthouse, and the locals.

Whatever you see of Cape Hatteras Island, where you look today; you must factor in the following: knowing that this used to be the second largest maritime forest north of the Rainforest in the Amazon region of Brazil. The Gulf Stream Forest.

The continent before the arrival of Columbus was covered with pristine forest land, covered in trees a squirrel could walk across without touching his feet to the ground, from the shores of New York to the inlands of Georgia. Domestic animals, introduced along with man, have trampled the vegetation and men have cut the forests to build and to export from the entirety of this eastern coast. All this in an attempt to recreate the Europe they were leaving. Whole forests of Europe were destroyed just to make one castle or monastery, and over the centuries, that continent ran out of trees. Here was a ready supply. The gold they sought turned out to be green in color. No one land was more mutilated than this island, known now as Cape Hatteras.

An authentic picture of early Cape Hatteras revealed miles of grapes on wild vines running through the scrub oaks, cedar, juniper, live oaks, and small pine in the stands of forests between villages. Magnolia trees grew wild, with dogwood, mimosa trees, and honeysuckle vines sprinkled throughout a floor of yucca, small palms and fern of all shapes. Blueberry and blackberry bushes were plentiful. The floor of the forest was covered in pine straw, and fallen limbs dressed in the green fur of moss. Intermingled on the floor of pine and cone were the white Indian pipes growing tall with coneflowers and buttercups, where streams of light broke through the heavy canopy of trees. Along the sides of the two track sandy roads were pink rosebushes growing wild and blankets of the red and yellow gaillardia flower. The dunes were covered in oats and green bushes sporting lavender and yellow flowers. Yucca plants displaying stalks of white flowers lined the sandy trails and roads near the beach.

This was the look of the island to the Croatoan Indians before exploration and population sold the logs and floated them across the Gulf Stream to build the structures of Europe.

The introduction of domestic animals: horses, cattle, pigs, sheep and goats, ate the tender shoots of trees and bushes attempting to grow back after one of the many seasonal hurricanes, and thus, over the years, vegetation was hindered from replenishing itself. Most of what you see are man made mistakes. Now, tall houses have taken over where simple greed and ignorance left off, once again, the forests and landscape has been destroyed in favor of civilization.

There has never been government concern about replenishing the beautiful forests of the past, and as the land has been stripped, wind and tide are finishing off what was once plentiful vegetation. Since the government has taken over, they have only been concerned with keeping the road open, and the commerce that visitors bring. There was no apparent acceptance of responsibility to nature. The latest craze is the care and feeding of birds, as the government encroaches on what was once the sustenance used for feeding the humans who lived on the back side of this coastal land. Civilization and special interest groups have arrived on Hatteras Island.

This island brings to mind cool breeze, lazy days, sweet ocean surround, and tranquility. This fifth and last volume, *Island at War*, tells the account of what this strip of sandy shore did in response to the need of protection for the rest of the country. To be a part of a country, one must be *a part* of the country.

The proximity of position of the island of Cape Hatteras, North Carolina, USA, caused it to be the gateway to the interior of major cities and government, which made it useful as a valuable defense for the entire country open to approach from an enemy. Therefore, first and foremost, all government military has been forced to take into consideration the protection of this outermost island bordering the mainland of America.

This book is set in the first six months of the German U-boat attacks off the island, during the entrance of the United States into World War II. As they are dealing with what the Germans called "Torpedo Junction, Graveyard of the Atlantic, The Great American Turkey Shoot", and more, the curious children are faced with war and what it looked like, revisit their family's involvement in the previous wars; from the first Indian War in the early 1700s through World War II, and the role their island played in each. In studying the involvement of the island in history one must be conscious of just how important a part Cape Hatteras played in the protection of all of America.

Their participation in war was never lauded with stone statues of great men, nor even mentioned the names of patriots, but since the number of patriots was the same number as island inhabitants, it would have been a daunting task. This island never was spared a war. We did not comfortably float through the years of conflict, unconscious of what was happening on the mainland; we participated and made it easier for the rest of the country to survive the war years. This island took more abuse from the enemy approaching our country in an attempt to conquer, than any other land mass that made up the mainland of the country. With the exception of the War Between the States, we took the brunt of the fight, and in most cases, gave as good as we got.

There were never any complaints, the steel resolve of an island was formed, and is still apparent in local families. It does take a special person to live on this glorious strip of sand…

In the opening paragraphs of the prologue, the island is described as it used to look.

Look at the island depicted in these books through those eyes. This is when it "was just us".

⋆ 1 ⋆

War

A sharp clap of thunder rattled the old stone house, followed by a short silence and another stronger thunderous crack. Everyone was awake and looking toward the windows for the lightening, or rain, that followed. There was none, only silence. At that moment Cap'n Charlie knew, so did Luke, so did little Blake. Ellie was awake but did not react as rapidly as the others until she heard the commotion in the hall. She reached down and grabbed her heavy robe and went to the door of her room, just in time to see her grandfather on the rise of stairs leading to the fourth floor. Behind him was Blake wrapped in his bed blanket and Luke in his winter coat. It was a cold January night, and the house only had one fire going, it was the nightly fire kept burning in the kitchen. This made the house tolerable until other fires were lit throughout the rest of the huge house. Since the kitchen was built separately from the rest of the house, should there be a fire, it could be contained away from the main house.

It was an unusual sound, and each recognized the subtle rumble of the shock sent throughout the southern part of the island. Most everyone on the south side was awake at this point. Eyes open, suspended breath. It

1

was the second night in a row. This night, everybody, even Nett, bounded out of bed, and rushed to the fourth floor to look out over the ocean. Here in Uncle Jabez's old office look out, they stood, Blake as close to his Pop as he could get, was leaning into him. Ellie on his other side, pressing closely to her grandfather, tears clouding her eyes, as the plumes of black clouds streaked with fire rose from the ocean, not even a mile out. There was so much smoke it was hard to see what was causing the sky to be so black, even at night, as the clouds were darker than the night. The fumes were so thick Charlie thought he could smell them. He reached around and grabbed the spy glass from the shelf where it always rested, as it used to be fun to watch ships going by their house on the hill. Sometimes they saw a whale or two.

This room was full of fond memories and history, as Sabra had used this vantage spot to track English ships coming close during the Revolutionary War. She was able to warn the patriots if any one of the vessels looked to make a run through the inlet at Ocracoke. With enough time, the blockade at the inlet was ready for them, thus this little outpost, high on the piney hills of Trent, was the first line of defense against attacks from the English, and necessary for protecting the island and cities inland.

This was different. What Charlie saw was a huge ship, split in half, with its bow raised out of the water and clearly in trouble. Men were scrambling on the deck, hastily lowering lifeboats in utter confusion. He saw one boat get hung up in the davit it was attached to, hanging loosely, resting on the side of the ship, completely tangled and too far from the water for the sailors (even if they had time) to cut the lines and let it drop. They just left it and went to help others launch another lifeboat. Moving the glass a little, Charlie could see as other men more carefully lowered another lifeboat, which, as he watched, hit the fiery water and burst into flames. He saw a man jump over, only to land in the pool of fire and disappear. The smaller fire from the burning lifeboat immediately joined the already huge flames shooting into the air.

The stricken ship began to sink lower in the water, and the destroyed bow, once angling upward, now appeared to be less and less visible as it drug the stern down with it. He lowered the glass, and shook his head, tears rolling down his cheeks. Blake looked at his Pop and motioned for the glass. The Captain refused. He did not want that image burned into his grandson's memory.

Grandmom waited, frozen in the bed; she knew she could not make the climb up to the tower, and really did not even have the desire to see the carnage. She thought that she never wanted to actually see what she was hearing. She quickly grabbed her glasses, robe, slippers, and a box of matches, and made her way down the dark stairs to the kitchen, lighting certain lamps as she went. If this was what she thought it was, there would be no going back to bed this night. Her heart pounding, she worked her way to the kitchen. Here she stoked the fire in the kitchen fireplace with kindling, then threw on more logs. She then moved to the old iron stove nearby and lit the wood to heat it up for cooking and left the oven door open to help her warm up the kitchen. Finally, she stopped shivering and began her task of making something hot for her family.

The five: Captain Charlie, his daughter Nett, her sons Luke and Blake, and Ellie, Grandmom and Grandpop's charge, all stood silent as the mighty ship burned. The Captain did not rush to call the Coast Guard, because from the position of the ship, just south of the Diamonds, it would be well visible from the station and he knew they would be already on their way to collect survivors.

The group huddled together watching the horrific spectacle, each at a loss for words, thinking their own thoughts, and all with tears welling up in their eyes. Nett was heaving sobs, with hands covering her mouth to muffle the sounds; she could not hide nor control the emotions she was feeling. Her thoughts were of her husband, Bill, where was he at sea, and was the same thing happening to him? She knew this was what it would look like if it did. She was devastated. There would be no surf men to go to his rescue, he would be alone, without the assurance that any lifeboats would be available, and if there were, how many would be saved? Bill was a mechanic, his position was in the belly of the ship, probably directly in line where the torpedo would hit. In her heart she thought he did not have a chance. She was sick. Luke put his arms around his mother, feeling her sobs, and trying to hold her together. He nestled his head at her side, and held on tight, trying to stop both their sobs. He too was thinking of his Dad.

Finally, Grandpop got his wits together, with an arm around Ellie, and another clutching Blake's little head close, he began to move them all down stairs, away from the spectacle of the fire on the ocean. Nett and Luke hesitantly followed, Luke not quite ready to tear himself away from that awful sight. Nett knew he was in shock, as was she, but she had to get him back away from the window. As the thick black smoke continued to rise upward, the fire gradually spread out over the ocean, the ship groaned and slowly began to disappear under the water, leaving a blanket of fire it its wake. Everything about the ship was now on fire, and it was so dramatic, it felt like they could also hear the hissing as parts of the fire not being fueled by the oil tanks on the ship began to sputter out, only to ignite again as the oil continued its spill.

Descending to the second floor and bedrooms, they could see lights on the first floor, and realized that Grandmom was in the kitchen. Only then were they aware that she was not with them. They went to join her.

Odessa was making biscuits; a jar of fig preserves and a slab of hoop cheese from the wheel on the side porch already sat on the long heavy wooden worktable stretching down the middle of the kitchen. From the kitchen, the ocean was no longer visible, and they could finally relax and give comfort to Nett. There were no words, only hugs and closeness, as they could not even offer assurances. What they had observed was the most fearsome sight any had ever seen. Each climbed on a stool Odessa's friend Mr. Con had built to fit her table, and still with no words, they all sat as Grandmom poured milk. She also had a pot of coffee for Charlie, he had responsibilities and she knew he was needed elsewhere.

Grandpop grabbed coffee and a biscuit and put a slab of cheese with one large fig on it. "Gotta go!" he said and rushed out of the room. Before anyone could answer, he was gone, biscuit in hand. Grandmom and Nett stood with their backs to the children, staring out the kitchen window at a slight glow across the way. The trees blocked the view, but both knew what they were looking at.

"Where's Grandpop going?" asked Luke, and he made a move to leave also.

"Get right back here son," Nett said in a choked voice. "Your grandfather is needed this night, he is probably going to the Coast Guard Station. I'm sure all the men are, there is much to be done, and if there are any survivors, it will take all of us to help. Just you sit right down!"

Luke sullenly took his place on the stool at the table, with his eye on the door leading from the kitchen. Then, remembering what his mother must be thinking, he said, "Mom, don't worry, Daddy will be all right." Nett moved away from the window and stood behind her son at the table. She pressed his head to her chest, and at that point, she, Blake and Luke hung their heads together, and silently cried. Blake moved his stool closer to his brother, and Nett returned to stand near the kitchen window. It seemed she could not tear herself away. Nobody noticed that Ellie was nowhere in sight.

Having followed her grandfather up to his room, she stood at the door with what she felt would be the proper hat for this weather. Her grandfather was fumbling with his clothes, and she could tell he was befuddled and dazed. When he turned to her she saw his red eyes, and she knew he was worried about this, about his sons, and about them.

"Honey, you go back downstairs with the others, I need to get dressed. I won't leave without saying good-bye." Captain Charlie said. "You need to help Aunt Nett, and you need to be next to your cousins. Everybody is hurting over what they just saw. But, you know we are going to be in for more of this, and we have to be strong. We are safe, and we pray that Uncle Bill and the boys are also." Captain Charlie was also thinking of Jack, and Curtis, in the Coast Guard, Wallace in the Pacific, and Fatio, the most in danger, as he was on one of those merchant marine ships most likely the target of the German U-Boat torpedoes.

"Now git ... you're keeping me from getting dressed." He crossed the room and gave his precious grandchild a tender hug, such a sweet soul, and so thoughtful ... she was always a comfort to him.

At that, Ellie turned and started down the hall, kicking an imaginary something, as she slowed herself down. She had to think, and somehow, in her thoughts, she saw Uncle Bill. He was sitting on a counter, in some kitchen galley, surrounded by other sailors, and they seemed to be smiling. The picture was enough to settle her a little, knowing that for this moment, he was safe. When she got to the kitchen, she leaned in between Blake and Luke and whispered, "Uncle Bill is not in danger." Both boys looked at her, with the knowledge that she *knew*, each spontaneously kissed her on the cheek.

Luke smiled at her, then at Blake, "don't worry," he said. "That's the last one you get," and he hugged her tight. *My cousin, the little clairvoyant*, he thought.

Just at that time, Nett turned around to see the affection between cousins. For some reason, seeing those three so close together, wiping each other's tears, she felt a warm feeling creep over her, something she could not describe. Contentment, relief... it was hard to describe the sensation, and she turned to her mother, seeing the same feeling on her face. Nett looked puzzled; Grandmom did not. As Ellie had gotten assurance, Grandmom's *knowing* had also kicked in, and calm took over where terror had once been.

"Nett," she said, "Honey, I have a strong feeling that Bill is fine right now."

Charlie came into the kitchen dressed for the weather, grabbed a couple more biscuits, and slapped some cheese and fig preserves on them, as Grandmom handed him some waxed paper, he covered them and shoved them in his pocket.

"O.K., boys, I'm going to the station to see what I can do to help. I'm stopping for Baxter, that blast was so loud, I'm sure he is awake. No telln', Bernice might be on his porch waiting for us. I'll be home when I can. Nett, I probably won't be in school today, tell everybody to just make do. I'll stop by White's house and leave a note on his door for Maude to cover my class and I'll be there presently." Maude White had previously served as principal for the school and was always ready when Charlie had business. "White might be waiting for me too. Dessa…can you fetch me some paper?" At that he followed his wife to the study under the stairs, got his notepaper, and gave her a kiss on the forehead.

"Charlie, Bill is alright for now, don't you worry." Odessa gave him a nod and quieted his heart; he knew she would know. What they did not know was whether or not the other boys were O.K., but both thought that Odessa would feel that also.

Grandmom and Nett got everybody back to bed, only a few more hours before daylight, maybe they could get some rest. There was no sleep to be had that night, but, the noise had ceased. The quiet seemed as deadly as the noise. Blake opened the curtains of his bedroom window to check on Theo, his wolf. He was in his usual place, on the porch roof, stretched out under Blake's window, making sure his buddy was not harmed.

It seemed that morning would never come, each child had spread apart the heavy curtains of their bedroom window in order to see the sun when it came up. Finally, they could tell it was time to get ready for school. Downstairs they could smell the comforting aromas of Grandmom cooking something, she had probably not even gone to bed. As they all gathered once more in the kitchen, there was an eerie silence, but at least this time they could swallow. Last night it was hard to get the biscuit past the lumps of fear in their throats. But this morning, they ate heartily, knowing there would be lots of activity and stories at school when they arrived. They couldn't wait to share what they had seen.

Nett told them all to ride their horses to school in case something happened and they needed to leave in a hurry. That very thing occurred a couple of days ago, when the U-boat had fired on a ship in the daytime. It had been with such force it made the windows look like they were melting, as they took the reverberation of the blast.

"Run children! Run!" The teachers had yelled, as they were afraid that glass from the windows would injure them if they broke. Most had walked to school, so running was definitely their only recourse. Luke, Ellie and Blake lived too far away to run, and they had quickly taken off for Uncle Tommy's house across the ridge. This time, they were happy to take the horses, so they would be prepared to come home to safety if necessary.

Everybody at school was all talk about the blasts from the night before. The U-Boat had struck an oil tanker on the south side of Diamond Shoals, as the ship tried to round the area in anticipation of the shoals. This was directly across from Buxton and possibly Trent, maybe it had even been seen in Hatteras, but with each village having their own community school it was hard to tell. The action seemed to affect Buxton most of all. Trenters also attended the school in Buxton, as theirs was the least populated of the villages. Most were delivered by a side railed truck with a canvas top. Mr. Charlie's kids usually came either with him or their mother, Nett, who taught grades one, two and three. This morning, the kids rode their horses. There was war afoot, and it made a difference in everybody's actions. The day went on as usual, with the teachers doing a masterful job of keeping the children calm. Luke saw his grandfather's ol' jalopy in the school yard when he went out for recess, so he knew his Pop had returned from the Coast Guard Station and would fill them all in at supper on what he had learned.

All three kids were glad their horses were tied in the woods in a spot that could be seen from the school window. More than once each would leave their seats to sharpen their pencils and look out on the horses. Luke thought this day would never end. Even though this was not the first time they had experienced the rumbling of a blast, something about the strength of this one was unnerving. Kinnakeet had experienced the same thunderous blast from a U-Boat attack days before, and the force was so close to the island, it had shattered the windows of the school. Pop said that the villagers at Kinnakeet could feel the murmur of the U-Boats charging their batteries during the daytime in anticipation of resurfacing for night attacks. The villagers could feel the vibrations under their feet, and for those who lived near the water, the disturbance rumbled the floorboards of their house. The U-Boat batteries were so loud, some thought that Kinnakeet kept a quiet hum hardly detectable all day. It could have been imagination, as the villagers were anxious knowing that terror was so close.

When the school bell sounded, all three of Cap'n Charlie's kids hurried to their horses, and with the same mind, they began to sneak their way to the beach. They were careful not to pass houses, because they knew Grandpop would find out. But, these kids were adventurous and curious, and had taken on scary situations before, so they were very careful and determined to complete their mission. When they finally got to the dirt path leading to the beach south of the lighthouse, they could see several men from the island still in the area. There was only one lifeboat they could see, but they dared not go any closer for fear of being spotted. So, they turned toward home. They did not notice the bodies stretched across the beach; blackened skin next to the white sand. Maybe they did, and just were not aware of what they were looking at.

Planes from Elizabeth City and Norfolk had been called to pick up the survivors, each finding a proper stretch of wide beach to land. The local men were taking care of the dead out of respect, worrying the circling birds would pick at them. They did not yet have body bags; the Coast Guard would deliver them as soon as they could tend to the living.

When the kids got home, they changed clothes and once again mounted their horses and went to the beach from the house. This time they were on the other side of the disaster scene, and seeing that the beach was clear, they urged their horses to the left side of the dunes to keep from being seen. They were riding near the ridge so that they could see over, but when they got to the wreckage, there were still men there, so they turned for home. After brushing down their horses they went into the side door to the kitchen where Grandmom was and sat at the table hoping for a snack. They were not disappointed. Of course, Grandmom had questions, but the kids did not have answers, they just related the day. Luke offered the information on Grandpop's return to school, and mostly, there was just small meaningless talk, if and when anyone spoke. It seemed that silence and thought were what everyone wanted.

At supper that night, they did everything but attack their grandfather for information.. The chatter was relentless, until Grandpop gave in.

"I left here, picked up Bernice and Baxter like I planned, left Miss Maude a note, Mr. White had already gone ahead to the station, and we were right behind. Several of the others who also do coastal watching were already there, so we caught a ride down the beach with some of the sailors. They had already taken the surf boat to the beach in anticipation of going out, hoping that they would be able to save some of the survivors from the ship. They got as close as they could, with the water aflame like it was, and pulled in about ten men covered in oil. Some were badly burned. The surfboat from Hatteras showed up, also the one from Creeds Hill. All of them pulled as many men as they could hold out of that fiery water. Each of the boats went out twice, maybe three times, until they were sure there were no more survivors or bodies to retrieve.

"Two of the lifeboats made it to shore, one of them pretty well shot up, but still able to float. They did what they could to get the chill out of the men, and everybody began taking survivors back to their stations in anticipation of getting them to hospitals in Elizabeth City and Portsmouth.

"You know, the water is deadly cold this time of year, and it wouldn't take much for a man to freeze to death in no time. Everybody was working against the clock to prevent that from happening. When I left the station, the men our guys bought in were still wrapped against the chill, and shivering. Looked to me like a couple of them might not make it."

While Charlie talked, Odessa kept a watch on his plate, his coffee, his comfort, as she seemed to be hurrying around taking care of the business of feeding most everyone at the table before herself.

"We are having a meeting at Eph's store tonight to talk about what we need to do here on the island to save the lives of those who are going to be hit next." Grandpop shook his head, and looking down, he said quietly, "tell you, this is the beginning. It is only February and looks like the Germans have their eye on shipping just off our coast. It is the perfect place to strike, as they all come through here on their way to the northern ports of New York and New Jersey. The Gulf Stream runs right past our island, at about a four mile per hour clip. Shipping is familiar with it. Now, the Germans are. I don't mean to tell you to get used to it, but our lives are about to change. I am looking at all of your faces, and I see fear. Rest assured, you will *not* be in danger, nobody is comin' ashore. Everything is going to happen out to sea, but as people who live on the banks, we have an obligation to render as much assistance as we can to help save lives."

Charlie swallowed hard, trying to relieve the lump forming in his throat. "We have kin in this, and hopefully there will be a helping hand when they need it. All of you understand, *you* are safe, but others are not. This island is no stranger to war. We have had to deal with every war the United States has fought in since the Revolutionary War. We are on the coast, front line of defense, we've done it before, and we will do it again. At least this time they are not comin' for us!"

He continued calmly, he needed to settle his family. "Now, I suspect from these three attacks over the last few weeks, we are gonna be in for it. There will be more and more military coming aboard this island, so get used to the strangers. This family left the lighthouse grounds just in time. We would have been in the way if we had stayed. Try to put this behind you, and get steeled against the next one, because this war might last a while."

"What the enemy is doing is trying to destroy Allied ships from other countries to prevent them from delivering supplies to the countries in Europe who are in desperate need of them. Now, those people *are* in trouble, their houses are being bombed, and in some cases the enemy is marching through their towns, but that is not us. Still, when they call it a World War, they mean that everybody is involved. So, we will do our part. And that means keeping calm and helping when we can. Just be glad they are not landing here."

"Pop, what is an allied ship, and has there ever been a war here, on our soil?" Blake asked.

"Well son, there are two sides, the Allies, meaning friends, and the Axis, in this case what we call the countries belonging to the enemy. We are an ally, or a friend to those who think like us, but are now under attack, so we are part of the Allies. We contribute to the side we have taken, and since the war is on a foreign shore, we send our help and our men there. We hope to never fight another war on our own land.

"Our first war in this country was the Revolutionary War, when we got our independence from England. It didn't affect this island much. The enemy, England, came over here to fight, and we were all involved in that one because we wanted to be our own nation, just like France and England are involved in the one going on now. And, even though this war is not here, it is in other places you would not expect, like Africa. Countries line up with the leader of whatever side they agree with. All of them thinking that at the end of the war their country will be bigger and will have control of more people. When one country decides it wants the land of another, war breaks out. We need to help our friends to keep this mess from spilling over to our shores."

Cap'n Charlie continued, "Another war fought on our soil was one we fought amongst ourselves, when the northern United States fought the southern United States. That was the worst, because everybody who died was an American. That is the only one where we fought each other."

"But Pop, why would we fight each other? I don't understand." Blake said.

"Oh son, not everybody is as content as we are to do what we do. We actually don't have the problems the rest of the country does. You might think that living on an island is terrible, but you will find that the more people you know, the more differences there are amongst them, and it makes for strife."

"What is strife?" The youngster asked.

"Trouble," his grandfather answered. "Let's just get through this one. We know how to do it, we had a taste of it just before you guys were born—same country, same greed, same area. That one was labeled World War I, this second attempt to gain land is called World War II. That time they didn't discover how to control shipping until the end of the war, when they arrived off our coast to sink ships before they got to their destination. But, before they could do too much damage, the war ended, and we were spared. This time it will be longer and worse, and like I said, we are in for it! But don't worry, we learned a lot from before.

"Remember General Billy Mitchell, Uncle Alaska's friend? Blake, I've heard you talk about him. Well, he got to surmising after the first World War, that we could use planes to attack ships, and he came to this island to demonstrate that very thing. He discovered this island because he liked to hunt and fish here; it looked like a good coast to work from. He sank two old ships right off Hatteras village, using nothing but an airplane carrying bombs. I'm sure that is what is going on right now across the water. One of the reasons we salvage iron, and metal, is because we are in a hurry to build planes, ships and our own submarines. For us, the new ships will help in this war against submarines. Once we get enough planes built, this island will be safe, because spotting subs from the air will even up the odds, and it won't be so easy for them to hide. Right now, the war has just started, and we were not ready, but you wait, this won't last long for us. The war will go on, but it will be over there, not here. Within the year, those underwater boats won't be lurking off our shores, because we will be bombing them from the air.

"Just sit tight, this thing is going to turn our way. Right now, this island stands between life and death for some men, and we intend to make it life. Now, enough with the questions, let me eat. It has been a long day for me, and I didn't get much sleep, so I need to get a little shut-eye before I go meet the others at Ephs."

The rest of supper, Cap'n Charlie tried to change the subject to something more in keeping with an easy digestion. He asked about school… about getting to ride the horses to school, just general things to get everybody's mind off the horrible thing that was happening to his peaceful island. In the back of his mind, he knew it would happen every night the U-Boats were here, and no tellin' how many. The Gulf Stream was the perfect shipping highway for states and countries to the south, and being located here, the U-Boats could destroy products from all the South and Central American countries, plus the Southern states. Unfortunately, he just couldn't prepare the kids for what came next. It was just too awful a thought to throw out there.

War! What a terrible thing to have to explain to your children. The whole time Charlie was talking, he could not wipe away the memory of what he had seen on the beach this morning. There were quiet times when his mind would not leave the possibility that one of those bodies could be his son, on some strange island, or burning up in the ocean, or going down underneath the water, and not being able to breathe. At those times, he was having a hard time breathing himself. His only joy at this moment were those three little ones, and the "funny" they added to his life. He had to get back to that, but not tonight. Tonight, he hoped to have a more restful sleep. God knows he needed it.

All down the Southern shore of Hatteras Island, other men and women were thinking and experiencing the same thing. Some were mothers who were alone, no husband or son to console them. Charlie sent up a prayer for them. It was the people who were alone he worried most about. He actually felt a little guilty to only have the problems he had, at least there were those he could lean on for comfort. He thought that after his nap, when he went to Eph's store to talk with the others that would be one of the subjects he would bring up…*we need to take care of those whose whole lives were left vacant by this monster called War that eats up people*, he thought.

The idea came to him that the community needed to provide comfort and hope to those they could identify who were having a hard time coping with loss and loneliness. He was thinking '*so far we have done a good job with strangers, but we must not forget about our own*'. He thought of the old phrase "*we are strongest in our most broken places.*" He could think of several women who were alone—their loved ones away in battle. Surely, they had also heard the blasts, and had no one near to console them. In his mind, he started at one edge of the village, and he touched every house up and down the road, making a mental list of those in need of comfort and friendship.

At that, he fell asleep in his chair in the office under the stairs.

★ 2 ★

Independence

Sabra Jennette Sargent was considered an island beauty. Unlike her mother, Rhetta, she was not a loner. She was slim, tall, and athletic, with blush red hair, the mixture of her red headed mother and blonde father. She was smart with a ready tongue. It was said she could sweet talk a fish up from the water and train a bird to her by simply extending finger. These traits must have been the ones she used when she stepped off a boat at the Hatteras docks on her trips home from school. She certainly used those skills to beguile young Billy Austin each time she saw him on the waterfront as she waited for her Uncle Jabez or his right-hand man, William, to fetch her with her baggage each vacation. Her boarding school, the Governor's Academy, in New England, was expensive and strict, and close to Harvard, which was exactly what Jabez wanted. She presented a striking figure standing with hair properly pinned up and clothed in matching frock and coat. Billy was ever aware when she was expected and was always there at the ready to help her with her trunks.

Most of the time she seemed as excited to see him as she did to touch foot on her beloved island. Immediately upon arrival she was whisked away to the Trent mansion, and there spent hours and hours in her mother Rhetta's sitting room laughing and giggling about whatever adventure she had experienced at school. Her stories pleased Rhetta, who was also schooled off island, as well as being presented to Richmond society as a teen. It was at the academy Sabra learned her skills as a horsewoman and proved herself quite the scholar. She had a flair for numbers and excelled in debate. She could stand her ground with any man, and usually did.

Sabra was adept in telepathy, reading the mind of others, one of the properties of being a Jennette woman, whose lineage came complete with one or more "gifts". This one was hers, and once she discovered the skill, she successfully used it to her benefit. Who knew if Billy Austin was one who was stricken unawares? Once Sabra set her sights on him, there was little he could do to resist. Later in life she would best any man in business, merely by using what she was reading in his mind to her advantage.

Billy was heir to the Austin trading docks in Hatteras, and when Sabra was home, she followed him around like a puppy. She learned business along with him and impressed his family with her aptitude for negotiation.

Sabra and Billy married, much to the disappointment of her Uncle who wanted a more polished suitor. But, alas, matters of the heart always prevailed and Jabez accepted her decision. He set out the mansion in its most elaborate splendor for his granddaughter's wedding. As a wedding gift, he had a beautiful chestnut colored Arabian horse, with a white mane and tail, tethered to a post near the porch for all to see. The stately beauty of the young colt almost stole the show from the bride. Upon seeing him, Sabra hitched up her wedding dress and rode him around the yard, to the delight of Jabez. Billy stood on the covered porch with the rest of the wedding guests and just shook his head—*what have I gotten myself into?*, he thought.

It had taken Uncle Jabez three weeks to find the proper mount, and the experience was the happiest he had been in a while. The search was a pleasant excursion for both he and Charles Jr., who each missed the adventures of their youth. There were no pirates involved this time, but they felt the familiar thrill when traveling around checking out stables while looking for that horse, as they had when they took to sea in search of booty to sell to the islands.

Sabra named the beautiful colt Journey.

Life for Sabra and Billy was the ultimate Hatteras style existence. They both lived in the village, near Billy's parents. Their house had a barn for the horses, and after a day at the docks, dealing with merchandise coming and going from the island, they always went for a refreshing ride on the beach on the south end of Hatteras. Here, they played like children, and Sabra collected unusual shells to present to Rhetta on her frequent visits back to her childhood home in Trent woods.

Eventually, Sabra gave birth to twin boys, Soloman Jennette Austin, and Jesse Meades Austin. She hired a nanny to take care of the boys while she and Billy expanded the business at the docks. There were many times when Jabez and Rhetta sent William to pick up the boys in order for there to be laughter in the massive house, and to give the young couple a chance to have some time to themselves. Their trips to the beach was where they seemed to do most of their business planning. Sabra was great at negotiating trades and at times, was the deciding factor in persuading a client to ship with them. Business men from the mainland were not so quick to say no the lovely compelling young lady.

On one of their afternoons at the beach, the couple was on their way back, when a rattlesnake spooked both horses, as it crossed the dirt pathway worn between the clumps of brush leading back to the village. Billy's horse reared up throwing him to the ground, and when the horse came down, he landed on his rider. Sabra galloped to the village for help, but was too late to help her husband, fatally injured from both the fall and the hooves of the horse.

Billy Austin's death was a blow to the entire community. His funeral spilled out of the little church into the road and yards of nearby houses, most of them "Austin's and Jennette's." Sabra took to her bed and became reclusive for months following. Her boys, being only four years old, did not understand, and were comforted by members of both families for the horrible days that eventually led into months.

Jabez and Billy's father were of the same mind, that this could not go on. They devised a plan to recover the lives their grandsons seemed to be denied. Jabez, knowing Sabra's energy, education and drive, suggested to Nathan Austin that Sabra be returned to the job she had taken on with Billy, and tackle it alone. They both knew it would be hard, but she was capable of handling it. Nathan and Jabez pledged their assistance should she need it. Nathan also was devastated by his son's death. His only consolation was still having Sabra whom he had observed as capable in all areas of running the docks. By the time they presented her with the idea, she was ready. Mourning was eating into her soul. In dealing with locals Sabra had a sobering effect. Many of them had entered into clandestine deals with Jabez during the pirate days and were not sure whether or not Sabra was privy to any journals he kept. Therefore, they were careful not to rub her the wrong way just in case she knew something about them that would adversely affect their own businesses.

Jabez and Nathan also decided that the boys should have a more stable environment and that Sabra should move back to Trent Woods to a house capable of accommodating the three broken hearts. They both knew she was lonely, and unhappy, and needed a friend. Who better than her mother? Rhetta was excited for the return of her beautiful daughter and happy to be in a position to help raise the two little boys. Jabez would devote the remainder of his life in the caring and teaching of Soloman and Jesse.

The mansion, previously shadowed with the death of Jabez's wife Evelyn, and Rhetta's loss of Royster, was now saddled with another tragedy, the death of Sabra's husband Billy. The Indian shaman Weroansquoa appeared to Rhetta in a dream, giving her confidence that spiritual guidance would always be a *meditation* away, thus lifting the cloud that seemed to hover over the Jennette family. Once again, the strength of the broken when mended, would prevail.

Sabra proved an excellent choice to further the commerce of the docks, she was the buyer, seller, and generator of one of the most important businesses in the village. When the country became embroiled in the effort to become independent from the harsh rules that stifled trade and commerce of the colonies, and from the taxes and rules not of their making, breaking away from England was the only answer. The British reacted with even more strict rules and punished the colonials with higher taxes on goods they needed.

No amount of trade interruption initiated by England, and heaped down on the rebels of the mainland, affected the island. Once again, the villages stood on the outside of problems experienced by the mainland. Instead of taking on the mantel of exclusion, the island entered the fight by being instrumental in supplying necessary products to the colonies who were experiencing the war first hand, on their own property. The island was especially helpful to the army, when destruction of farms and supplies became critical, and food was scarce. It seemed no amount of British suppression dissuaded the rebels in their struggle. When the British once again delivered heavily taxed tea to the mainland, the ports of New England resisted. Loads of tea was dumped into the harbor as protest, leaving the rest of the colonials, who were fond of their afternoon drink, without a way to continue the trade.

It was a well-known problem which Sabra felt she could remedy. She learned from the elders of Kinnakeet village just how to manufacture and package the yaupon leaf. It was a type of holly tree that grew wild in that area in such ample supply, that it sorely needed harvesting.

This unusual plant, with sweetened leaves growing abundantly on the island, was used in several ways. Indian warriors applied it in religious ceremonies to purge and purify themselves, being careful to avoid the poisonous berries. The leaf possessed high anti-oxidant properties similar to blueberries. Sabra knew from Rhetta and her connection to the past, the many qualities of this small tree that grew in great quantities on the island. In Kinnakeet, along with other locals, she built a factory to dry the leaves and package them for tea and sale across the sound in larger markets. The leaves and twigs were chopped fine, then layered in large barrels with heated ballast stones to dry them, once dry, they were either transported in bulk, or packaged for brewing tea.

The tea proved profitable to the island and was even consumed in the Governor's mansion. It provided a necessary substitute for the tea once prized from India. Both abundant and healthy, it was rich in polyphenols helpful in the prevention of degenerative diseases, particularly cardiovascular diseases and cancer. Specifically, it also had an anti-inflammatory effect. The pirates brewed the leaves for consumption in an attempt to ward off scurvy. The tea proved to be unaffected by any change in packaging and storage, similar to green tea. It became the substitute for the tea being sold by the British, who imported it from their own factories in India, making as much profit from colonial dollars as they could. The replacement tea became quite popular with the colonies, surviving even past the war. The added advantage was the unexpected wealth the colonies reaped. It was one of the first substitutions for British products successful in the newly fledgling country.

Hatteras, during the interim to all-out war, also boasted another attribute; the mainland found the island was needed in the fight to sustain themselves without British help. The island could supply fresh meat necessary to feed the colonial armies, as the position of the Hatteras docks and capable pilots to navigate the sound, insured unencumbered delivery to inland North Carolina and Virginia.

Sabra and Jabez became quite a pair in the conflict. In Jabez's study on the fourth floor, they used the window facing the sea to observe passing ships. It was easy to track English ships sailing the coast as they searched for an unprotected harbor to invade in order to reach inland colonies, for fighting, stealing, and commandeering young men to press into service of the King.

Because the coastal islands were covered with an abundance of cattle, sheep and hogs, the British were a constant nuisance to the locals, as they steadily attempted to land small craft ashore to steal fresh meat. Occasionally they attempted to kidnap young men for service to the British crown. It kept the locals on constant vigil to protect themselves and their property. The shallow channels of the Pamlico Sound protected the mainland, and the shoals were only known by local pilots. The shifting sands of the Pamlico Sound kept intruders from entering and unless led by the knowledgeable locals it was folly to even attempt to navigate the shoals. It also prevented commerce from leaving, inhibiting the ability to trade. Not everyone was in favor of the British; both France and Spain stood to gain if the colonials won. It was at this time the colonials learned to be excellent blockade runners. Most of the inlets to larger cities and towns near the ocean were already blocked by British ships, but here, they did not feel the need to blockade since the natural shoals of the sound prevented ships from getting out. Locals proved them wrong.

Also, a thorn the British had to contend with when attempting to stop activity through the hole opened up by the shoals of the Pamlico Sound was the inclement weather that plagued the seas around Hatteras Island. Once again, the closeness of the Gulf Stream to the island allowed frequent storms to inhibit egress into the island and beyond. Most of the time they were incapable of carrying out a raid, or strike against colonial shipping because they could not fight the weather that constantly whipped up the seas around Hatteras and Ocracoke.

Most of the trade of North Carolina and Virginia was moved through this pocket. The British were determined to plug the inlet that lay between Ocracoke and Portsmouth Islands, leading to the interior of the states. It was a steady fight, as the British did capture numerous merchant vessels off the Carolina coast, however, the most they could accomplish near the inlet was stealing cattle and hogs, or sheep. The islanders fought back, even without the necessary war implements to protect themselves, bravely they foiled many a raid on the island. Their resistance remained a sore spot for the British as nothing seemed as easy as it looked. Seeing the bounty and obtaining the bounty proved close to impossible. The islanders were also fighting for their livelihood. The colonials gave as good as they got, as they even overpowered some smaller vessels, like the *Lilly* and the *Polly,* and transferred them to Edenton, North Carolina, for Colonial use. Ocracoke pilots took another British tender carrying 1,000 pounds of gunpowder and kept sixteen prisoners.

Another island commodity in the fight for independence was salt. The harvest from Hatteras Island was instrumental in filling the steady need, as they collected it from both sound and sea. Finally, the mainland colonials recognized the advantage of protecting the products coming from the area through the inlet between Ocracoke and Portsmouth Islands, allowing the locals to continue to more freely supply needed materials like salt, meat, tea and protection from enemy landings to the over matched rebels. Locals kept vigil nightly against raiding parties, hiding in the dunes, beating back the raiding parties and capturing their weapons.

At one point during the war, Washington himself at Valley Forge was dependent on the trade and supplies coming through the area of Cape Hatteras Island. His men would have starved without the food from the island delivered through back channels.

Sabra stood in front of the windows on the fourth floor and watched as the English warship sailed south too close to shore to disguise their intentions. She knew it was headed toward the inlet at Ocracoke, in hopes of gaining entrance to the inland waters of North Carolina and Virginia. Beside her was her grandfather, Jabez Jennette, and they both were of the same mind.

"Sabra, hand me the spyglass." Right away, Jabez knew what to do. "Send one of the boys to fetch Abner." (Abner was William's grandson, who did work around the barn. He was good friends with Sabra's boys and the family treated him like another son.) Sabra found Jesse in his room and sent him to fetch Abner.

Abner rushed up to the fourth floor where Jabez and Sabra were tracking the British ship with the spyglass.

"Son, we got us a possible visitor." Jabez handed Abner the glass and pointed him in the direction of the ship. "She's English, right? O.K., you get up that pine we use to signal, take one of the mirrors up there, and signal the harbor to get ready. Now son, you keep signaling till they give you a flash back, to assure that they saw. Won't be long, I know they have somebody on duty. Then come on back here and finish whatever William has you doing. Looks like we'll have a little excitement tonight. William and I will take you boys with us this evening to watch the fun. Take my horse."

With a big grin, Abner raced down the stairs and out to the barn.

"Why couldn't I go, Uncle Jabez? I can climb faster than Abner, I know cause we've raced up that tree before." said Jesse.

"We need you here to keep a watch on that ship; let us know when she turns, and signal Abner when she does. Your mother and I are taking the wagon to the docks. I'll be back later to fetch you boys and William. Somebody's got to watch that ship." At that Jabez and Sabra left to get the wagon and horses ready. Hatteras docks were about an hour away, and time was wasting just looking out the window.

Even though the country being embroiled in the war with England had involved the island as well as the mainland, so far, the island was only in danger when ships came too near. Cape Hatteras successfully blocked the entrance to Pamlico Sound, leading directly into other rivers and waterways, thus denying access to both North Carolina and Virginia cities, New Bern, Bath, then up the Roanoke River to Virginia, reaching the towns of Portsmouth and Norfolk the back way. The inlet between the islands of Portsmouth (NC) and Ocracoke were the only way to get into the mainland of North Carolina, and the back way into Virginia.

Other islands only protected one city at a time, but the Pamlico was fed by other large rivers merging into the interior of the sound and thus allowing access to larger and more important cities. Already the British had stopped traffic into and out of the Chesapeake Bay, but this was the second way to enter, with a much smaller opening, not so easy to control. The shoals were deadly and caused enough larger ships to go aground that the British stopped trying.

Access allowed the supply route to the patriots at war, so Jabez's hilltop mansion was the lookout for anything threatening to attack from the sea. There would have been no reason for a ship to bombard Hatteras; heavy fire would only kill a bunch of cattle, as the villagers lived on the back side of the island. Jabez was now an old man, and his adventurous days were over, this new assignment as "look-out" was exciting to him, as it kept him active and in touch with danger.

Sabra was involved also. Her tea factory, the salt factories up and down the island, and trying to protect from British raiding parties stealing meat was a full-time job.

She was especially intent on signaling local blockade runners who attempted to bring in or carry out supplies, or trade with both other coastal cities and opponents of England whose sympathy stood with the colonies. These local pilots were invaluable to the colonials, as this was their sailing grounds, and they were comfortable in avoiding the shoals that so plagued the enemy. Her outpost was most familiar with the "runners" and they depended on her line of sight. The system of mirrors Jabez had set up was valuable to their success, and to Jabez, it was as exciting as anything he had ever been a part of. He imagined himself as once again with the pirates, and when approached on the docks, gave the younger men necessary advice on the ways of operating in covert situations. He was most respected, his pirate trade legendary, and what he could no longer do as a young man, he could do as a seasoned expert. Jabez provided essential insight into clandestine ways that had been perfected by himself and others he had known. He had met the enemy and knew how to avoid them.

This new outlook on life gave Jabez pleasure, and with the care and nurturing of his grandsons, he found himself once again a happy man. One thing he did not realize was the value of protection Rhetta's wolves afforded his dwelling. Jabez had hogs on his property, and for some reason he never was in danger of a raid by the ever encroaching British on his property for meat. He also wondered why, knowing of his lookout position, clearly seen from the sea, they did not try to destroy his house. What he did not know, but should have, was the pack of wolves was ever present surrounding the house on the hill. Rhetta's wolves had historically been protective of the property for more than two hundred years, this was their home also and they had, on several occasions, stood as sentries with barred teeth and low growls when confronted by the enemy sneaking through the woods to access and take out the tower. The whole raid looked easy until faced with a wolf or two, or more! It was annoying having seen the hogs, with this house so isolated from other homes, they were never allowed to get close enough to steal even one.

Sabra's boys, unknown to her, were introduced to the wolves by their grandmother Rhetta, and though they were not lucky enough to have one as a personal protector, they learned not to be afraid of them. Mostly, the boys were more familiar with their mother's business at the docks, and as a result were quite close to their father's family, the Austin's. Unlike Rhetta, or Sabra, they did not go to school in Buxton, they went into the village of Hatteras each morning with their mother and were more familiar with that village as an Austin. Though the boys were helpful at the docks, and quick learners around the vessels, they were quite a handful. It was always easier to get in trouble when there were multiples, counting Abner among their accomplices.

They were typical island boys, and without the constant supervision of their mother, or grandfather, sometimes got themselves in trouble.

Once they were aware of the British ships sending men ashore to steal from the locals, plus, hearing the stories on the dock of locals hiding in the dunes to ward them off, they decided it would be quite an adventure to do the very same. One night, along with Abner, the boys left the house after the grownups had retired and made their way to the beach with bird wings stuck in their hair like the Indians, to ward off evil. They waited for something to happen. Nothing did. They were so disappointed not to have an adventure story of their own, they kept up the charade for several more nights. Each day at school, they were so tired they fought falling asleep in class. Finally, one very dark night, they observed movement near the shore, and spotted a dingy being hauled up on the beach. At this point, they realized how scared they were, and made so much noise running away that it alarmed the thieves, who quickly retreated, thinking it was a band of angry locals come to kill them.

Of course, the story told the next day at school was far braver than the truth, and for a bit, they were the talk of the school. This story was also told at suppertime around the table full of grownups, and eventually got back to Sabra and Jabez. It was the first time these boys were punished. Jabez stepped in and restricted their leaving the property for a week. He even threatened the "switch", and his anger was so obvious the boys were taken aback. They decided to find other ways to entertain themselves.

Once this story was told and retold throughout the island, other spirited island boys, not to be outdone, began to act up, and as a result, the activity in the dunes at night exploded into quite the commotion, which in fact deterred more than one raid.

Both Nathan Austin, and Jabez Jennette became fast friends because of their grandchildren. The combination of the skill in contracting and managing shipping that Jabez possessed, and the workings of the docks familiar to Nathan, made for a profitable shipping business operating off the Hatteras docks. That trade stayed strong throughout the history of the villages of the island. The hub of shipping around Hatteras was enhanced even more once the inlet was cut in 1846, moving inlet trade, from Ocracoke, to Hatteras village.

Though only minimally involved, the villages of Hatteras Island were instrumental in their role of successfully winning the war for independence against England, as much as any battle in a mainland town or politically organized effort by the rebels to obtain their freedom from a tyrannical, controlling government. Seemingly left out of the War for Independence in history, this outer island was in fact, an integral factor, providing support that could only have been furnished by them. Lacking a proper arsenal, supplies to the army were as necessary as weapons, and having participated in that way turned the tide in many battles that would have otherwise been lost.

This outlying island did participate and was an instrumental factor in the securing the country's independence. The island, located thirty miles off the coast of mainland United States, became, in this first war, a recognized necessary value to the whole of the country. As time went on, it repeatedly stood between victory and defeat, as it protected the inland cities of a growing nation.

War of 1812

This time it was Blake who went to Grandpop's encyclopedia Britannica to learn as much as he could about the first real war fought by the now United States. He read all that he could and found nothing about any involvement by Cape Hatteras when relating the facts of the colonies fight to gain independence from England. Even as the sound of destruction that carried through the sea air each night pounded their ears and disturbed their sleep, he was determined to find out if this was how all wars were experienced. Each night they heard the explosions of torpedoes hitting ships, and each night, depending on how near or how far it reverberated, Grandpop would leave his bed and rush to the Coast Guard Station near the lighthouse to offer his help. He was always tired during the day, and as he continued to manage the school, he began to take long naps in the afternoon to regain his strength.

Grandmom and Nett constantly cautioned the children to be careful about noise, lest they awaken Grandpop, asleep in the big chair of his study. It seemed that everything made a noise. If they went to the horses, their neighing might awaken him, or any roughhouse playing in their rooms, directly over his study, was a bother. It began to be a stressful time for everybody, as tiptoeing around the house got old fast. Collectively, the three began to think of things they could do that would not create a bother to the grown-ups of the house. The war outside on the ocean created tension in the big house, and they could not seem to get away from it. They realized there were only two places they could go that would be acceptable. The third floor, with all the books, or the caves. Another detail they realized, was that nobody looked for them. As long as they were quiet, nobody seemed to care what they did. So, they began to spend time in the third floor attic where all the trunks were located.

Each afternoon, as Grandmom busied herself in the kitchen, and Nett in her quarters, they used their individual secret places to access the stairs. They found that the best plan was for all of them to use the ladder in Ellie's closet next to the wall of her grandparents' room, as Grandmom's quarters were seldom occupied. On the other hand, Nett was frequently in her rooms, next to Luke, making Ellie's room the perfect spot to gain entrance to the attic without drawing attention. Most of the time they indicated that they would be in the little cottage, or in the barn, or in the boathouse, when in actuality, they were pouring over old trunks in the attic. Whenever Grandmom would retreat to her room for an afternoon nap, or to write letters, they quietly went to the fourth floor, and using the door of the fireplace, they went between the walls down one level and into the room from there. They always spent only as much time as they dared, not wanting to get caught by being late for supper and having someone look for them.

It was always in Ellie's mind that Grandmom *knew* where they were at all times because, everybody's location was something she would have *known*. Grandmom had *the knowing*. Ellie couldn't tell if Grandmom's gift was stronger than hers, but it seemed to be pretty strong. Grandmom also confessed one time that Weroansquoa was a frequent visitor in her dreams, so, Grandmom definitely possessed knowledge far beyond anything Ellie had ever told her, and at times, she was there for comfort when Ellie was having trouble with her own "*gifts*". Ellie, having the same *knowing* ability when she tried, did not insult Grandmom' s psychic intelligence, and just assumed that she was allowing their secret getaways. As long as she knew they were safe, she would not give them away. The boys, on the other hand, just thought nobody knew, and felt comfortable in thinking they would not be discovered, thus betraying the room with all the magic.

Blake started going through the wooden crates and trunks in search of any more journals that Uncle Jabez might have stored there. After going through several, and Ellie scolding him for not putting everything back where he found it, he began stacking papers in a more organized way, so that he could return the piles as he had in the exact way he had uncovered them.

Luke came to his rescue. "Ellie, why be so hard on him," Luke chimed in, "it's not like anyone else is ever going to know, or even come up here to look." His priority being to search for anything he might find from one of the twins. Surely, they had discovered the room, and he thought that maybe Rhetta, their grandmother had told them. It kind of made sense, to her but by that time, Ellie's harping was having an effect on Blake, and he started to do it the way she wanted in order to avoid her side glances. He respected Ellie too much not to do as she instructed, he knew better, but, he was so carefree, he did not take offense. Being the youngest had its drawbacks; he was just glad to be included, even if it was being scolded. At least they were paying attention to him.

Ellie was searching the girly trunks for clothes, jewelry, or drawings from Rhetta, anything she could find that would interest a girl. She really wanted to know what Sabra's school in New England was like, but there seemed to be nothing from Sabra. At last, she found another journal written by Rhetta and settled near the window to read; at dusk, putting it properly back in the place where she had found it. All the while, sneaking a peak at Blake, just in case he was checking up on her as she had done to him. She was sorry she had complained because she found it was not as easy to return items in their exact place, but she kept up the pretense, and at least looked like she was following her own advice. In the end, she felt badly for scolding Blake, and slipped over next to him as he was organizing his mess.

"Blake, I'm sorry I was so cross, when I was going through Aunt Rhetta's stuff, I realized it was not so easy to put things back exactly the same. Sometimes I can be too hard on you. Don't be mad, I'm really sorry…friends?" And she stuck out her hand.

They did a handshake, and all was forgotten.

The journal Blake found was unlike the "Magic Book". On this one no colors showed up, and he could only read, not *see* the stories he was reading. He read the information about the island's participation in the revolution for independence, but it was written like a log book, with entries about shipping, and ship sightings.

He liked the account Uncle Jabez told of the boys getting in trouble sneaking down to the shore to hide among the sea grass, in hopes of making so much noise it scared off the boat coming ashore. It gave him an idea. The whole thing looked like great fun to him, and he thought how easily he could do the same thing.

He didn't really know if there were any Germans pulling up to the beach at night, but, he thought, it wouldn't be a bad idea to find out. He thought of how fun it would be to leave the house by his window over the front porch, and shimmy down the huge live oak whose branches almost touched the house. Those branches had been cut back so as not to actually touch the roof, for fear of squirrels or other varmints getting into the house, so they were not spindly, but rather strong, plus he had already accessed the tree from his room when just fooling around. The only thing he had to remember in his attempt to be undetected was Theo, who slept right under his window at night, and would not take quietly to being stepped on. Yes, he had a plan, and was definitely not going to share it. He didn't think the others would be interested anyway. So, he began to plot out his new adventure

One afternoon, Ellie read in one of Aunt Rhetta's journals that Uncle Jabez had died, right after the Revolutionary War, and Rhetta went on and on about what an interesting and exciting life he had led. They all stopped reading at that point, and just sat where they were on the floor of the attic in silence. Ellie just looked out the tiny window at the sea, and was deep in thought, remembering. Blake looked at Luke and knew what he must feel like, his heart broke for his brother. He was correct, Luke really was the most affected, he truly felt like Uncle Jabez was his friend, and the adventures he had with him and the pirates, felt almost real. It took him days to want to return to the trunks after that. It was as if he was in mourning, and he couldn't share it. Blake thought he heard Luke's muffled cries that night in the room next to him. Blake always kept his closet door open to Luke's room. Luke didn't but Blake did. He just felt safer, the noise at night from the U-Boats and their firing on passing ships always made him uneasy, as it did everyone. Most nights the thunderous firing was on the north shore, nearer the lighthouse, not in front of their house as before. Because the island was shaped like an elbow, there was what the islanders called "the north side, Buxton, and the south side, those villages south of Buxton, Buxton being at the elbow." The terminology was not entirely correct, but it made sense and reduced the explanation to the fewest words. No matter where the noise originated, Blake just felt safer being able to be closer to Luke.

At supper one night, Blake asked his Pop if he knew anything about the mainland wars that involved the island. "Pop, I know about the Revolutionary War, because we learned about it in school. Mr. Austin told us about the way his family was involved in helping out selling supplies to the mainland."

Grandpop was sort of tired about all these conversations centering around war at the supper table. He felt like the war going on right now was about all the thinking he could do concerning the subject. But he did understand the interest of his youngest grandchild and his need to know, also, who better to ask than the man he always thought knew everything about everything.

His teacher, George Austin, was one of the locals who went away to college and returned back home to teach. Blake's "Mr. Austin", would know a lot about how the island responded in the Revolutionary War, because some of his kin had been involved. The Austins had always owned and operated the docks at Hatteras. "Son, Mr. Austin would know for sure about that because I believe his family was involved in helping out in the war."

Grandmom, who never got involved in most things, interrupted, "Charlie, did you know that the Austins are distant kin to my family, the Jennettes? I believe they might have lived in this house during that war, because one of my ancestors was married to a boy in the Austin clan who died young, so she moved back here with her sons because her mother lived here. They might have been the last ones to stay here for any length of time. But, as I understand it, Sabra's boys always kept a watch over the place. Most of the time it stood vacant, until they turned it over to my great grandfather who deeded it to my grandfather, who was a Jennette. This old house has always been in the family, even when others stayed here, they were always connected in some way to the Jennette's. I really wish I had paid more attention to my ancestors, they were evidently interesting, but, someday." Grandmom's voice trailed off as she seemed lost in thought.

The three kids heads were on a swivel about that time, looking at each other and kicking each other under the table, making eye contact, with Blake screwing up his face at Ellie, like he had something to say. Meanwhile, his Pop continued. "Nope, I didn't know the Austins had anything to do with this place. I always thought, since it was deeded to you, that it was only occupied by that old pirate who built it, and maybe a couple others. I never knew of anyone to live here except somebody in your family. Dessa, I also never knew you were distantly related to the Austins." Charlie looked a little surprised that there might be something he did not know about Dessa.

Quietly, under his breath, Luke said, for only Blake to hear, "he was not a pirate."

"Actually, I don't think I am related," Grandmom continued on, "but I think somewhere down the line some of my kin were."

"Well, me being from Kinnakeet, I didn't know much about your family till I met this sweet faced filly from Buxton." At that, Charlie gave her a wink, Grandmom blushed, and the kids, along with Nett, observed the affection they had for each other. This was one of the few times they had been privileged to see their grandparents show endearment. It was always understood, as Grandmom was all about "her Charlie," but it just was so natural they never noticed. Once again, the side glances, and Blake's little giggle let everybody at the table in on the secret…his grandparents were still very much in love.

"Anyway kids," their grandfather continued, "seems like it was your grandmother's family that had the yaupon factory in Kinnakeet, which supplied the mainland with tea, after the Boston Tea Party."

"I know about that Pop!" Blake blurted out.

"We all do, goofy! You act like none of us have ever been to school, what you need to know, is that you are always the last one to learn stuff." Luke was getting irritated with Blake's constant questions, he was more interested in what his grandfather was doing each night after supper, when he went to join the other men at either the general store or the Coast Guard Station.

"Now son, those are pretty harsh words for your brother, he can't help it if he is curious, and I think it is great he pays attention in school. Don't be so hard on him. Just you wait, in a couple of years he is going to catch up with you in size, and never can tell, he might whip you." Grandpop chuckled at his remark, but Luke looked sullen.

"That'll be the day," he said, "yessir, that'll be the day." Luke puffed up his chest with his arms cocked in a threatening way and moved toward Blake playfully to indicate he was the better man. Ellie punched Luke in the arm and gave a smile and a giggle at Blake. She had seen more than one shoving match between the two, and Luke always let Blake win, always.

Grandpop easily slipped his chair back and placed his napkin on the table indicating he was finished with his meal. "Don't mean to be rude, but we'll talk again tomorrow night, I need to retire to my study and get a nap before all the commotion acts up tonight. You fellas keep on eating, don't mind me, I just need my rest. Can't take the chance of falling asleep in front of my students." He motioned to leave, and Grandmom stopped him.

"Charlie, I made a blackberry pie tonight, don't you think you might have time to have just a tiny piece?" She jumped up and hurried down the three steps to the kitchen, bringing back a beautiful pie, still hot, evidenced by the towel she had under it to keep from burning her hands. She knew that he could never turn down a dessert, and in her mind, she also knew he would get himself another piece when he came back tonight after his meetings. She could just see him sneaking into the kitchen for a slice before going to bed.

"Well, just a small piece," he said, "never could turn down pie." This being blackberry season, how could he refuse? He grinned at the boys and gave a little wink.

After he left the table for his study, Grandmom reminded the children just how hard he worked, and how many jobs he had, and they should be careful not to tire him more than was necessary. "You know you can always ask your mother some of these things, she is as smart as anybody in this family, and I'll bet she can answer some of your questions." The kids all looked at each other, they had never thought about their mother knowing anything.

Days passed, the U-Boats were relentless, averaging two attacks a day, and it began to almost be normal. But some evenings the kids could not help but ask questions, sometimes of Grandpop and now, sometimes of Nett. They discovered, surprisingly, that their mother knew quite a bit about the history of this island, and their admiration grew almost to amazement. Who would have ever thought that your mother would know anything? For a couple of nights, the ocean was quiet and grand pop was allowed to get a full night's sleep. On those days, the family would gather in the big living room while Nett played the piano and they all sat around and talked. With music in the background, the boys would again question their grandfather about history. This one night it was questions about what happened after the revolution, the second time the island was faced with war against England. Of course, it was Blake who chose the subject; Mr. Austin was now on the War of 1812.

"Pop, Mr. Austin said we went to war with England again after we got our independence. Did they really burn down the White House?" he asked.

"Yep, it was around the same time as Theodosia Burr was lost off our coast. Ellie, this might interest you; the British never did get over us whipping them and throwing them out of the country in gaining our independence. They always thought if that war had lasted a little longer, they might have won, so when we started acting like a real country, building our own ships and trading with the other countries on our own, they found themselves in competition with us for trade. That didn't set well with them. Plus, we only had the thirteen states, and there was still a lot of land here to conquer and claim sovereignty over, so they always looked at us like they could come back. They were trading with the Indians, in competition with both us and the French, and they were over here all the time. The French had the same idea. Nobody looked at us as having any power, and they acted like it. Sort of like you look at Blake, Luke, you always think of him as your little brother, and sometimes you boss him around."

Grandpop gave Luke a little scowl accompanied with a smile.

"Oh, Pop, I don't really think that way, he's really my best friend," and at that Luke grabbed Blake by his head and gave him a 'dutch rubbin,' ruffling up his hair with his knuckles. Blake looked all embarrassed, knowing it was true, there were no better friends than he and his big brother.

"Well," Grandpop continued, "on the ocean, when we came in contact with the British, sometimes they would stop us, board the ship, and if any sailor had English kin or ties to England, they would take them to their own ship and press them to work for England. Kind of like kidnapping. The British were also at war with the French about that time. The English were trying to supplement their navy with American sailors, and so many countries got involved, it might have also been called a world war, as the Europeans were going after each other and taking sides. We got stuck in the middle, because there was so much land for the taking in this country, we could hardly keep up. Greed is a terrible thing, and all this unclaimed land on this continent was eating up those in Europe who had run out of free land. It didn't help that the French sold their part to us, to pay their debts. So, the race for the rest of this country was a scramble. If countries wanted more land, they had to fight each other or come over here and fight all over this land. Both countries tried to explore and claim lands west of here that were not already part of the United States, they even drew in some of the Indian tribes to side with them and had them fighting each other. It began to be a problem. Finally, we had had enough, and war was declared against the British, and here we go again!"

"It was during that time that Theodosia Burr, on her way from South Carolina to Washington to see her father, was lost at sea. Her ship, the *Patriot*, washed up on shore at Nags Head, without any people on board. Some say, the British were responsible, but not likely. There were internal problems in Russia and others blamed them, and also Pirates were suspected, but nothing was ever proven. Quite a mystery that was. Her husband, the governor of South Carolina, even sent papers with the Captain of her ship, the *Patriot*, which explained, if they were stopped that this ship was a passenger ship and did not carry contraband, and, was not involved in war."

"What is contraband?" Blake started, as a cuff across the head by Luke shut him down; Luke was trying to follow the story.

"Quit it!" He said crossly.

"LUKE!" Grandpop gave him a stern look and he snapped around as his grandpop scolded him for picking on Blake.

"Anything that might help us, like guns, or money to buy guns," Grandpop answered. "You know, they might have been right, as later word was that they carried both in the ballast of the ship. But it is an old story, and there is no way to know the truth. It just became part of the war.

"The hate the English and French had for one another really caused this little country a lot of trouble. If they had not been fighting each other for seven whole years before our revolution, maybe the English wouldn't have needed to raise our taxes and treat the colonials so poorly. In that war, the French jumped in to help us, you know, anything to hurt the British, and created another problem at home, sending France into a bit of a money crunch. Seems the wealthy try to get more money from the poor, and it caused the poor people to revolt against the rich, like we did, and it just seemed like problems in Europe were spilling out all over the place. England tried to push us because France was pushing them, and it was like nobody was satisfied with what they had, and it kept boiling up everywhere.

"Everybody thought they could solve their own problems if they had more land, and the extra land was here. So, you've got a period of the French fighting the English, then us fighting the English, then the French fighting each other, then back to fighting the English, and the English trying to make up the slack by fighting us again to pay for fighting other people. Got that…? Like I said, greed, that's what war is all about, somebody trying to tell somebody else what to do."

"Wow Pop, and here we are again, with them fighting over there, and it is spilling over on to us, and we don't want to fight anybody." Luke was all ears at this point and with a big smile was realizing just how complicated anybody going to war was.

"The French were having a hard time for a while, in all their turmoil, an upstart named Napoleon named himself Emperor and vowed to take over the world. But that didn't last long. The English put a stop to that. We were lucky, only some of their ambition was aimed at us."

"I've heard of Napoleon; how did he get into it?" Blake thought he had another hero.

"Thank goodness Napoleon was stopped before he ever got to us. He is another story entirely," Pop said. Now the Captain really had a headache. If war on the ocean outside his window wasn't enough, he had to tell the history of war to his kids, and tell it in a nutshell.

Grandmom stepped in to stop it. "Young-uns, if you open your mouth with one more question for your grandfather, about ANYTHING, I'm going to send you to bed right this minute. If your Pop doesn't have a headache, I do!"

Then Nett chimed in, "and here I was going to tell you about some things your father was doing, and I feel like I'm still in school. All of you…get upstairs, right now, you hear me, right now. No more talking, no more waiting for a nightly snack, no more of anything, and you bring this stuff to one of our peaceful family gatherings ever again, and you'll rue the day!"

As the kids hopped to it, and started scrambling to get upstairs, Luke was draped across a chair Ellie and Blake at their grandpop's feet, all seeing who could get up before getting smacked on the head. But, the only thing Blake could think of was, "what is true?" He knew better and concentrated on beating the others to the top of the stairs, knowing that the closet doors would be open, and they all three would settle it without the grown-ups. Boy was everybody mad. THIS was WAR!

When they were safely upstairs, and huddled together in Blake's closet where all the blankets were, quietly talking about what they knew, and what they wanted to know, Ellie reminded them that on the night Theodosia Burr had flown her over the ocean to see the wreckage of the

Patriot, there was a terrible storm raging in the area, so the stories of storms keeping away the British was correct, she had seen it.

The following day, Blake raised his hand, and determined to get his answers, he began on Mr. Austin. He wanted to know about burning the White House. He got his answers and then some. Mr. Austin told him that one of the greatest weapons this area of the country had against invasion was the weather. Apparently, when the British tried to use our inlets once again to get access to the mainland cities, there was a terrific hurricane preventing them from getting anywhere near. So most of the action was north of us. In that way, our specialty was blockade running; we were skilled in the ways of pirates, whose methods were effective with enemies at sea. We provided protection against British raids into the mainland and also a base of operations. American privateers built up quite a reputation for stopping ships and stealing whatever they found of value. They were the outlaws against the organization of war. The British were structured, and the Americans were sea bandits, with no laws or rules to hinder them.

Mr. Austin also told them something that really fascinated Blake. It was during this war, when the British came ashore and burned the Capitol building, the White House and other Washington buildings. At the time there was anchored off the coast, in a Baltimore harbor, a British ship. On that vessel was an American lawyer, Francis Scott Key, who was attempting to obtain the release of prisoners of war. He watched in horror as the British turned their guns on the U.S. Fort McHenry in the harbor. As the fort burned, Key wrote his poem, later to become *The Star-Spangled Banner*, the national anthem of the United States.

One famous American privateer was the Snap Dragon, carrying four twelve-pound guns and a pivot gun. In the first seven months of the war it captured ten vessels, took 150 prisoners and one million dollars in cargo. The Americans were learning exactly how this thing called war was played.

Even during all that, storms kept on coming. Regardless of the country of origin, ships met their fate, as usual, on the tides of an angry sea. The schooner *Independence* was wrecked in a vicious storm off the coast of Kinnakeet, carrying much needed sugar and coffee. Only one man was saved. This island seemed to have built in protection, as the storms raging up the Gulf Stream always created a natural deterrent. Still do. Unfortunately, it is now mostly a hindrance rather than a help.

Blake was full of it on the way home from school after all his questions had been answered. He couldn't wait to tell Grandpop, and he was hoping to get it done before supper, as he remember the warning from the night before about talking war at supper. The kids were all bouncing around in the car with Nett, talking "birthday" with him, and teasing him about "presents".

"You better say what you want Mister," Nett said, "after last night it might be switches," and they all laughed. "Grandmom wants to know your favorite cake, you can rattle it off, and see what ingredients she has. You know no chocolate, we can't get that because we don't have any more rations for that. We do have enough sugar, Grandmom's been saving for this."

Blake thought and thought, "I know! Banana pudding cake!"

"Nope, no bananas." Nett wrinkled up her nose. She did not want to deny him what he wanted, but there was no choice.

"O.K., I guess it will have to be lemon meringue pie cake!" He seemed so pleased with himself.

Nett didn't have the heart to say that wasn't a cake, she decided she would tell her mother to make a lemon cake. She didn't know if that was a thing, but Mom would know, and if it wasn't she would make it up.

That being settled, Blake was still naming off things he wanted, most of them impossible, but none of the kids could ever remember a bad birthday, so they just listened and teased about pine cones, coal, a rock with his name on it, and it got sillier after than that. Luke had gotten him fishing boots, Ellie was giving him a beautifully carved small horse. She and her grandmother had asked Mr. Conn to whittle it out of a piece of black cherry wood he had left over from another project. Ellie was so excited knowing how much Blake treasured his figurines from Mingen, and this one was Spirit. Nett had the best gift of all; a new colorful blanket for Spirit's back. Grandpop had plans to take him to the Coast Guard Station the next time he went, of course Luke would go also, knowing Blake wouldn't have enjoyed it without him, Grandmom's was a surprise. Blake couldn't wait for the weekend.

They pulled up to the house and everybody went in except Blake, he was going to wait on the porch for a private conversation with his grandfather when he came home. It was Cap'n Charlie's habit to sit on the porch after a busy school day and smoke a couple of cigarettes, just to wind down.

"Whatcha doin', buddy, you're gonna to freeze to death." Luke came back with his coat still on and sat down on the swing beside his brother.

"I have something I want to tell Grandpop," he said, "and I'm not supposed to tell him in the house."

"Mind if I wait with you?" Luke started swinging, and Ellie came out.

"What's going on? You guys got some secrets?" Ellie squeezed herself in between the two boys, and gave them a threatening look, like 'ready or not here I am!'

Then Nett came out putting her coat back on, and wanted to know what was up.

Grandpop drove up and wondered what the heck everybody was doing on the porch on such a cold day. He looked at them all and sat down in his favorite rocker and took out a cigarette. "O.K. what's up?"

Blake looked at everybody with his special weird look. "Grandpop, I wanted to talk to you and all these people came out here, I don't know why."

"Well son, here I am, what is it?" Grandpop took a drag off his cigarette and blew a smoke ring into the chilly afternoon.

"Don't get mad at me Grandpop, but I just wanted to tell you I have all my answers about the White House (and adding in his inside voice), I don't know why they are here." Grandpop smiled, even serious Blake was funny. "But, Mr. Austin also told us about the Star Spangled Banner. You said no talking about war at supper, and Momma said not in everybody's company, and I wanted you to know; 'cause I thought you liked our conversation, but they are all butting into my business, and I wanted you to know that too!" Blake said in a matter of fact way, throwing in a little attitude.

"Son, I'm glad you had fun in school today, sorry I was so cross last night." Grandpop blew another smoke ring, "Well Luke, did *you* learn anything in school today?"

"Yup, I saw Mr. Hathaway and Freddy Beal get in a fight, 'cause Mr. Hathaway makes Freddy sit on the front row 'cause he's so mean, and nobody wants to sit on the front, cause Mr. Hathaway spits when he talks. When he spit on Freddy, Freddy jumped up and pushed a desk at him, then Mr. Hathaway chased him around the room, and Freddy pushed another desk, and Mr. Hathaway went after him again and Freddy jumped out the window, screaming "you ain't spittinn' on me no more!" and out the window he went. Mr. Hathaway screaming, "Beal, get back here! Beal!"

It would be hard to describe the shocked look on Cap'n Charlie's face, or the surprise on Nett's, but all Grandpop could say was, "anything else?"

"Well," Luke said, "Mr. Hathaway only has one suit, and he's fat, and starting to stink."

There was silence, then everybody fell over laughing. Grandpop laughed so hard he got to coughing, and Nett had to slap him on the back. So much for relaxing on the porch. Cap'n Charlie thought maybe he'd better ask about school more often. The vision of school from the student's view was like a comedy show.

THE STAR-SPANGLED BANNER

From a poem written by Francis Scott Key
"Defense of Fort M 'Henry"

O say can you see, by the dawn's early light
What so proudly we hailed at the twilight's last gleaming
Whose broad stripes and bright stars through the perilous fight
O'er the ramparts we watched, were so gallantly streaming?
And the rockets' red glare, the bombs bursting in air,
Gave proof through the night that our flag was still there;
O say does that star-spangled banner yet wave
O'er the land of the free and the home of the brave.

On the shore dimly seen through the mists of the deep,
Where the foe's haughty host in dread silence reposes,
What is that which the breeze, o'er the towering steep,
As it fitfully blows, half conceals, half discloses?
Now it catches the gleam of the morning's first beam,
In full glory reflected ow shines in the stream:
'Tis the star-spangled banner, O long may it wave
O'er the land of the free and the home of the brave.

And where is that band who so vauntingly swore
That the havoc of war and the battle's confusion,
A home and a country, should leave us no more?
Their blood has washed out their foul footsteps' pollution.
No refuge could save the hireling and slave
From the terror of flight, or the gloom of the grave:
And the star-spangled banner in triumph doth wave,
O'er the land of the free and the home of the brave.

O thus be it ever, when freemen shall stand
Between their loved homes and the war's desolation.
Blest with vict'ry and peace, may the Heav'n-rescued land
Praise the power that hath made and preserved us a nation!
Then conquer we must, when our cause it is just,
And this be our motto: 'In God is our trust.'
And the star-spangled banker in triumph shall wave
O'er the land of the free and the home of the brave!

Ellie's Dream:
The Sea Fights Back

The sounds of war disturbed the sleep and waking hours of the island. No village was exempt. By day, the villages located on the eastern bank, from Kinnakeet to Pea Island, felt they experienced a constant vibration under their feet, as the low hum from German U-Boats charging their batteries for the night time carnage, either real or imagined, it was unsettling. The boats only had about six to eight hours of submersion time, and at night, they spent the entire six hours checking their periscope or equipment screens for any sign of shipping on the horizon. In the early part of 1942, the Islanders had not yet realized, nor had they been told, that the lights of the village served to silhouette the passing ships, like a backlight screen. Not until almost three months into the war did the Navy shut down all the lights on the island, including the Cape Hatteras Lighthouse.

Houses needed to darken their footprint by installing heavy green shades, or blankets that shut out light completely. They were adamant about cars and flashlights. Everyone either painted over their head lights or taped them so that only a slit remained, just enough to follow the road. On moonlit nights the islanders did not use lights at all. In addition to dark, the island went silent. People did not talk about what they were seeing or hearing anywhere except in person. No mention on phone lines, as all phones on the island were on a party line, and it was never clear who was listening. Newspapers avoided any mention of submarine news in the area. They avoided alarming the cities near the ocean. The motto, "loose lips, sink ships," was never clearer than among the villagers on Cape Hatteras Island. If one had relatives across the sound, or on the mainland, they did not write letters about what was happening here. There was definitely no mention of shipping expected, sighted, names of ships passing the island, or ships destroyed off the coast, even though the names of the stricken ships were known, the islanders did not repeat them, as they were actively trying to rescue survivors, and keep with the idea that knowledge was confidential.

Little Blake had found a dead whale on the beach that day, and thought he recognized the pattern of white on his skin. He came home crying at what the war was doing to their friends who lived in the deep waters off their island. He thought about what they must be thinking, as dead human after dead human floated down from the surface of the sea. Surely there were other creatures dying as their mangled forms drifted to the bottom. He and Spirit hurried home as darkening clouds over the water indicated there was a storm coming.

As Cap'n Bernice had once said, "if you want to know the weather, just look out the window."

Blake was becoming a quick study of the weather and took pride in paying special attention to the old men of the island talking about it. He wanted that same knowledge. He studied the skies, the stars, and the wind to help him in his understanding, and wanted to someday be able to predict the weather just like his grandfather did.

The secrecy the islanders were forced to keep was creating pressure on everyone. It seemed that during the day, people were tense, and at night, they were unable to sleep as each torpedo awakened them, and the second, or third, guaranteed they would not sleep. Most men rose from their beds and went where they thought they could best be used. This all happened from January through July, until the United States was finally able to manufacture and put into action enough ships to provide convoys to protect the merchant ships sending supplies to the war effort.

The entire nation was collecting iron for the effort. People went to work in plants making war machines, ships, planes, ground vehicles. Everything was used for the war. Islanders even searched beached ship-wrecks from years past for the iron that could be salvaged.

It was decided by those involved in the war effort that news of what was happening here was an indication of the enemy being off our shores, and that knowledge might cause undue stress or panic. The mainland was not informed of U-Boats sinking ships off the North Carolina and Virginia beaches.

It was that night, with the discussion of the whale, that Ellie was most disturbed. She tried to sleep but could only toss and turn quietly in her bed, saying the 23rd psalm over and over, until finally she fell into an uncomfortable rest, then, a very deep sleep. Normally, when she was having a hard time cutting off the events of the day, she would watch the beam of the lighthouse as it passed her window every seven seconds. When she counted the seconds between beams, it did not take long for her to fall asleep. However, there was no beam on this night to comfort her. Most of the time she never got to the end of the psalm, or got confused and had to start over, finally just dropping into a deep slumber. These days, she had to resort to her silent recitation more often, but her mind had gotten used to the message, "put this tiny head to sleep," and after only a few words, her inside voice recognized the chant, and just let her go.

During this deep moment, her mind went to the ocean, and she dreamed of Iris, James and Willie swimming near the shore, each time a wave came in, the dolphins were more flamboyant in their antics as they surfed the huge waves whipped up by the storm. Finally, she awakened Blake, then Luke, and all three left their beds, and were standing on the shore, looking out over the fitful ocean. The kids were so upset at what was happening to their beloved island.

It was March, and a heavy nor'easter was predicted to pass over the island.

Ellie and the boys stood on the shore, leaning against the wind that was kicking up white water, and sending lacy interlocking fingers farther and farther up toward the dunes. Peering intently into the sea, the kids could see their dolphin riding the second set of breakers in perfect tandem to each other, as they appeared to wait for their riders. The storm was getting stronger as Poseidon rose majestically from the ocean floor. His blue hair, flowing wildly around his shoulders, was matted with tiny shells, sparkling like diamonds as the water from ocean spray and rain bounced off them. He was angry that he was being used as a companion to the vehicle of war that his ocean was now. In his right hand he brandished the three-pronged trident, signifying his power over storms, tsunamis, hydrology, earthquakes, geography, and bringing down lightning and thunder, meteorology. His face was clouded with anger. He was determined to protect his dolphin, and his legacy. He looked like he could holler down the clouds.

He hurled the crystals on the sand near where the three stood. Ellie picked up hers, and the crystal thread began to cover her body, as she bravely walked into the roaring sea. Iris swam near changing colors with each crash of a wave. She dipped under to allow Ellie to climb on; the thread completing its task of fashioning a saddle for her to mount. As each child picked up a crystal, the threads quickly formed a suit. The children could hear the squeal of their dolphin over the roar of the storm, as they followed Iris's lead. Holding on tight, the storm pushed back against the surge, but the dolphin appeared to welcome the challenge. The three were riding the waves of a very strong nor'easter.

Ellie was awakened by the flash of light brought to her window by the bolt thrown by Poseidon. She realized there really was a storm, and she sleepily smiled as the dream reassured her that their pets were not harmed. Sleep came more easily now. When her eyes closed, the dream continued…

The creatures of the deep knew these children, and knew the honor bestowed on them by Poseidon. The sea began to fight back. Poseidon threw a mighty bolt, followed by a heavy crack of thunder which warned the ships of the impending fight. The ships moved farther out to sea, to avoid the storm which was darkening the sky. That got them out of harm's way. The order on the U-boat was to surface at all cost, as the power of the waves were moving them in directions they did not intend to go. But as they looked at their instruments, something on the water was emerging that put fear in the entire company, as they became aware of sharks, by the hundreds waiting for them to break the plane of the water.

Meanwhile Poseidon, in a mighty roar, hurled a lightning bolt that broke through the surface of the water and carried down to the undersea vessel, setting off sparks inside the instrument panels and frying their equipment. Behind that came a wave that curled from deep in the ocean with the mightiest force, striking the sub to its side and moving the huge tonnage like it was a toy. This was followed by another force of water that hit again. The boat, having lost its ability to right itself with instruments, was then at the mercy of the sea. It was like a sinking ship, without benefit of correction. All of this, as the might of the waves the sea god was creating, caused the U-boat to roll over and over in a virtual spin.

At this point, there was so much destruction and filth inside the tight quarters of the sub that any recovery would halt their mission. They feared they would have to return to their bases in Germany, if they were lucky. Poseidon calculated it would take days for the enemy to recuperate and be ready to continue their carnage. This length of time, he figured, would serve the Merchant ships well, and give them a slight respite from the dangers which would once again begin.

The children were safe on their dolphin and watched as ships moved ever east to avoid the Diamond Shoals and get to safety from the force of wind blowing against them from the north and the east. The storm, though troubling, was actually saving lives, as it forced the unprotected ships farther

into the ocean to the east and away from the enemy. U-Boats knew there
was a storm, but, in the past, were less affected under water, however, even
though the weather was removing all shipping above them, to less tempestuous
waters., they found themselves so stricken and so shattered that continuing
appeared impossible. At this point, the Germans had been so disrupted they
had no idea how to reconnect to their task of search and destroy. For this day
the war was halted, the enemy confused, the ships safe, and the dolphins had
taken the kids to see it all.

The merchant ships had been doing their best to avoid torpedoes before the
storm interfered. Now, although they did finally have depth charges, the men
were hurriedly learning how to use them against the missiles fired at them. The
victims carried stacks of barrels loaded with explosives and programed to destruct
at various depth levels. They usually carried around six to ten barrels at the
ready, with more to be stacked and moved to the rack as needed. It took several
attempts to learn how to place them correctly in order to damage a submarine.

The barrels needed to explode near enough to the subs to cause confusion,
hopefully enough to encumber the firing of the torpedoes. The depth charges
were not as dangerous as the missile but when they came close, inside the
sub, instrument panels shook and broke, gages were thrown off their measure-
ments, but loss of life was seldom a factor. If, however, there was a direct hit,
or two charges landing on opposite sides of the submarine at the same time,
it would cause the sub to buckle, causing serious leaks, and, that would be a
finishing shot. But the odds were with the U-Boat.

All these explosives were killing life in the ocean. After the whale was hit,
it did not take long for the leviathans, and dolphin to avoid any area that
carried an unfamiliar sound underwater. Poseidon had also had enough; at
this very moment, he was whipping up the wind and water to inhibit the
strange metal riders on the ocean.

The storm forced the enemy to stay submerged, but, they found themselves
being tossed about like a plaything. Their destruction of intended victims was
halted. The U-Boats could only stay under water for less than eighteen hours,

and then only when moving. They could not sustain the buoyancy for longer than that and had to surface. In a storm, they were tossed around like all other solids riding the water. However, most of the daytime, the U-Boats traveled above water to stave off the effects of stale air, and tight quarters. They wished the storm to subside, they had never before had one which affected them so destructively. The sailors were now sick and with an entire boat to clean, they wished for a sunny day, and wondered if they would survive to see it.

On sunny days, they set out to sea, away from shipping, and sun bathed on the deck of the sub. For a moment, these formerly normal men were released from their hideous task. On those days, they were careful not to be detected, there was no danger from the air, as the U.S. was still trying to keep up with the need to build both planes and ships. When war came to the United States we were not prepared, it happened to us, and we played catch-up for months to protect ourselves. The U-Boat attacks took place at night, when the Germans could see ship lights, or the ship, if silhouetted against the land. On this day, they doubted if there ever would be another attack.

Ellie awoke at the third sound of thunder and the sharp crack of lightening that followed. Her dream interrupted, the weather still raging, the rain and wind beating on her window, she covered her nose against the cold. She felt better, even though the war was still out there in the ocean, this storm whipped up by her hero, Poseidon, and her dream let her feel more comfortable that the pets they rode into the ocean, were all staying safe.

The children had always been fascinated with mythology, and they loved the names of the deities they read about. They were also a product of Weroansquoa, who seemed to honor spirits they had never heard of, also Powwaw, the shaman. These were characters in their heads, and although they worshiped and prayed to the God of the Bible, they had compartmentalized these book figures into a separate place of honor, and with all that was going on inside their minds, everything had its place. They knew they were of exceptional linage, and these were those spirits that looked after them. There was no "worship" of Poseidon, but there would be no denying that they believed he existed, but only in their minds. He was a hero, a flawed hero, but no less than any other one they knew, just as they loved the comic book character, Superman, this was no different.

Finally, morning came, the storm was still actively tearing apart trees and scattering loose materials in the yard, but at least they could look at it. Grandpop had called off school, as some places on the island would be flooded, and he did not want children out in this weather. He did not practice closing school every time it rained, but a nor'easter was just below hurricane weather, and sometimes more destructive, and he did not want anyone to get hurt by falling branches.

Grandmom did not awaken the children, she intended to let them sleep, but, to the man, they were all downstairs sitting like little birds with their mouths open waiting to be fed. She smiled, *not a lazy one in the bunch*, she mused, and began whipping up pancakes; a treat on a blustery day.

Grandpop was already gone, out to the station, or down to the grocery store, meeting with the other men, making sure everyone else was taken care of. The noises of the storm were much more pleasant than the now familiar sound of an enemy strike. Still, with all the activity of late, it would be necessary to make preparations ahead of time for when the war started up again. They had learned where they should prepare, they had gotten 'caught short', at times without the proper provisions on hand to take care of the wounded, and this would be a day to fix that.

The kids were upstairs in Uncle Jabez's study, then downstairs in Pop's library, looking up all the things they were curious about. With the storm still raging, the single window in the attic did not give enough light to hang out there, so they concentrated on other problems they thought they needed to solve. They imagined the fury of Poseidon, as they watched the physical evidence of his anger raging across the ocean.

After looking in books all morning, they spent the afternoon in the barn with the horses. It was a cold day for the barn, but the horses were in need of care, and since the kids considered them a part of the pack, they paid close attention to their welfare. They imagined the wolves had a safe place to stay, as they had not seen them since a couple of days before the storm. Surely the creatures had anticipated the bad weather and had found a protective place to ride out the wind and rain.

Finally, they went back to the house, and totally bored by this time, they went to the large living room and cranked up Uncle Fay's victrola. They sat with their books and listened to a record their father had sent them of "Puss in Boots and other Tales of Mother Goose." On their bellies, with a fire raging in the fireplace, the kids stretched out amongst a pile of books they had pulled for the afternoon and listened and read.

Nett passed by and observed the mess on the floor and reminded them that what they pulled out they must put back. That put a damper on an already damp day, but the admonishment did not last long, and they figured they would clean up, when they finished…and kept on reading.

When Grandpop came home, they followed him to the kitchen to hear the news of the day as he related it to Grandmom, but it was all so boring they went back to their books. They played "Puss in Boots" again, and Blake fashioned himself the *Marquis of Carabas*, and swash-buckled himself all over the room, swiping at this or that, till he finally broke a small figurine on a low table near the window. Ellie put one hand on her heart, and the other to her mouth as she reacted. Blake rushed to the kitchen to tell on himself, and all was made right with the world. They could not wait for the weather to change so they could go outside. They had been inside for two days, and already, they were getting antsy. They hatched a plan to explore the caves.

Since it was winter, Ellie thought that creatures she wanted none of would be somewhere else, and hopefully it would be warmer. At least if there was still rain, they would not get wet. So, the caves it was, and Puss in Boots raged on, saving a child, getting in trouble, pilfering things that belonged to the evil Marquis and to their fascination, speaking with a French accent. They were delighted that it was a French fairytale and giggled at Blake's imitation of a French nobleman.

Grandmom cooked a stewed chicken with dumplings to overcome the cold with a hot meal. Ellie, a known fan of dumplings, ate until she felt she would have a stomach ache. Blake spent the whole meal in the character of a Frenchman, and the war was temporarily forgotten.

Operation Drumbeat, as the Germans had named the war on coastal Atlantic, was also waiting for the weather to clear, as they too cranked up a ship to shore radio and listened to Benny Goodman. They also called themselves the wolf pack, which would have highly insulted the children who considered the wolves their friends.

Sometimes they called it the "great American turkey shoot", named so because of the ease in which they carried out their goal of taking out supplies headed for Europe, in desperate need of rubber, from South America, oil from the Gulf, and copper from Chile and Peru. The heroes of the war in the beginning were those who served in the Merchant Marines. They faced more danger than anyone, as long as the U-Boats were in operation off the coast, they were the target. Without convoys to protect them, they found it necessary to pilot themselves to safety by avoiding the areas where they were most vulnerable.

In 1942, most of the fighting for the armed services was in the Pacific, against Japan, who had attacked the United States first, in Hawaii. The Germans, though having declared war only four days later, were marching through Europe on land. Their sea war being carried out by U-Boats, seven of which were assigned to the war off Hatteras, and found it such a mark, that more boats came. For seven months Hatteras Island was a battle ground, it seemed like it would last a lifetime. The kids were scared that the enemy would come ashore, but they did not express that fear, since everybody had their own fears and there was no need to add more.

The storm eventually left the area, and since it was Saturday, the kids were almost stir-crazy from staying cooped up inside and decided to take their horses down to the beach. They intended to check on the light-house. Always, after every storm, the lighthouse was their main concern. The horses needed the exercise, and even the wolves were tired of hiding. The weather was cold, February being the 'snow month', it had been cold for all creatures, so they were all glad to get out. Now, as March rolled around, there was the possibility of the yearly nor'easter that always accompanied this month, and it did not disappoint. The weather was almost welcome, as it stopped the thunder of torpedoes from the ocean… As they were leading their horses out of the barn, a low whinny sounded, as Ol' Tony and Big Roy were also stiff and needing a little exercise, they were reminding the kids not to forget them. They were immediately led out to the pasture, with a promise that a stretch of the legs would follow the very next day. There were just so many horses they could handle at one time. The ride down the beach was fun, the sand was packed down hard from the rain, and all six wanted to go at a gallop. They were unaware of the eyes looking at them through binoculars.

It was not the first time the Germans had observed active horses on this island. But it was the first time they had noticed children riding them. Usually, it was a man on horseback, and they had seen that many times, as the entire beach was patrolled by the Coast Guard, or the Navy, on horseback. They had begun to track these riders and their movements, on the chance they dared to come ashore for provisions without being detected by a rider. The horse could smell them, so it was really taking a chance. They needed to know exactly when it was safe to land in one spot or another.

This appearance of children on horseback gave them pause, they certainly could not afford to be detected by children. Plus, these chil-dren seemed to have also brought along their dogs. Dogs were more of a problem than horses or people. Little did they know the 'dogs' they were looking at were actually wolves. Now that would have given them a start! This was quite an interruption of plans. They had already picked out several members of the crew who spoke flawless English, without a German accent, which more than anything would give them away. Unbeknownst to them was how they were going to stand out on an island whose dialect was so strong that most 'strangers' could not understand them. Now, seeing this new activity the enemy needed to rethink their plans. The articles they needed from shore would have to wait.

Meanwhile, the kids, unaware of any danger, as the sea looked worn out, played their way up the south beach to the lighthouse. They encountered a lighthouse sitting in the middle of a rainbow, with vivid distinguishable colors. This was the brightest one they had ever seen. Even the sky was glad the storm was over. Luke thought it was interesting that the rainbow was at the lighthouse. On the trip up the beach, Blue and Ellie had gotten ahead of the others, and from behind, Luke could see a rainbow over Ellie's head. It seemed to be a ring of colors surrounding both she and her horse Blue. He hurried up and caught up with them, only to discover that there was no rainbow at all. But, when he got to the lighthouse, there it was again. He would have to figure that one out later. It was not the first time he had seen distinct colors above Ellie's head. Most of the time however, the colors were only blue and silver. This more colorful arrangement was new.

He felt he should pay more attention to his cousin, she was a fragile soul, and growing up, they had all been careful to not let her get hurt, on the chance they could not stop her blood from free-flowing from a wound. As they got older, they thought she had grown out of it, but in Luke's mind, these new colors might have been a sign to him, that she was still fragile.

The new colors surrounding Ellie did mean something. Neither she nor Luke was aware of just what the change was. Yes, Ellie's dolphin, Iris, changed colors, and now, these colors were somehow connected to Ellie.

When they stopped their horses next to the lighthouse, they rode around the back, so as not to be seen. There was activity in both the keeper's house and next door in the assistant keeper's lodge. None of the people were ones they knew. They even thought that some of the men of the village might be there. The kids certainly did not want to interrupt any secret meeting. Their snooping and listening days were over. There were too many things going on that were far too grown-up to be taken lightly.

They let their horses rest, comfortable that the lighthouse had survived the latest storm, but they dared not stay around any longer. One thing they noticed was the debris washed up from the storm, there was so much it covered the formerly white pristine sand. They wanted to rummage through it, as it had washed up all down the stretch of beach. Mixed among the shells were the signs of decimation. Lives and ships lost, oil, tar, big hulks of wood and metal objects, even a torn up lifeboat. The beach looked dirty.

This eastern coast of the island did not look normal. They had seen glops of tar and oil beginning to show up as they neared the point of the island, so they turned inward, nearer the dunes, to keep the horses from getting it on their hooves.

Luke, Blake and Ellie just sat on their horses and looked around. Something was wrong with Ellie, she seemed flushed. Maybe the cold air had been too much for her, sickness was just below the surface with her, and the boys usually were aware of the signs, but this time they had been too busy.

"Ellie," Luke said, "You all right?"

"I don't think so, I feel like I should go back. I need to talk to Grandmom." Ellie looked first flushed, then pale, and both boys were now worried.

Quickly, they turned their horses and went the inside way back to the area just below the point. When they hit the south beach, Luke made them all stop.

"Ellie, let Blake take Blue's reins, and get behind me, I am afraid you might faint and fall off, and I don't want you to get hurt. We have to get you home."

Ellie dismounted, and handed Blake the reins, she grabbed Luke's extended hand, and with Blake's help, she mounted up behind her cousin. Luke could tell just how sick she was by how tightly she grasped his waist. And, when she rested her head of his back, he knew she needed Grandmom. He gave Gus as much speed as he dared, and they all hurried back to the house in Trent Woods.

At home, both boys stayed close to Ellie, as Grandmom tucked her into the bed.

While Grandmom went to heat up some soup, the boys sat on the bed and just stared at their pale little cousin, hardly peeping over the covers. She said nothing, just closed her eyes, and was asleep in an instant. Grandmom came with the soup, but just let Ellie sleep. She questioned the boys on what happened, but they both said that nothing happened. Finally, Luke told Grandmom about the rainbow just around Ellie's head. Surprisingly Grandmom smiled and shooed them all out of the room.

"She's going to be all right, don't you worry. I can fix this." Grandmom stayed and put the back of her hand on Ellie's forehead. Fever.

Ellie's dreams were feverish, and she seemed to be seeing things in front of her. She also felt the presence of a strong wind, and unconsciously pulled the covers up even tighter. The wind was not cold, it was just out of place. She thought she saw her mother, then the shape changed to Sabra, then the familiar face of Weroansquoa came to her; she gently put her hand on Ellie's sweating forehead. She pushed back her hair and leaned down to place her cheek beside Ellie's cheek.

"*Ellie,*" she said softly, "*you are not sick, you are beginning to come into your powers, I think the first one is extrasensory perception, or second sight, meaning you should always listen to your inner voice. It is sometimes called "intuition". If you feel something strongly, you should believe in it. This way, you can keep your cousins straight. They will listen.*"

Slowly, Ellie's eyes opened, she felt stronger.

"*Today you will also be granted,*" she paused, "*the gift of Telepathy, the ability to speak with your cousins, or, an animal, or whomever you concentrate on, through your thoughts. You have been demonstrating that with animals, but if you think hard enough, you can send your thoughts to a human, your cousins to start. You should practice on them. These talents you are getting now because you are in need of keeping your family safe in this time of war. This one you will need right away."* Weroansquoa continued, slowing down between each gift, to allow Ellie to grasp what was happening to her.

"There are three more, Pyrokinesis, *the ability to manipulate fire;* Hydro-kinesis, *the ability to manipulate water, and the last one,* Mediumship, *or channeling, the ability to communicate with spirits. You have already toyed with some of these, but you were not aware of what you were doing. Now, you need to know."*

Time passed, the blue and silver light stayed. Travis stayed.

Weroansquoa, once more put her hand on Ellie's forehead. It was cool. She was a little girl, these were mighty talents, and she was struggling inside to accept the gifts. It was exactly this that had weakened and eventually killed her mother. When the gifts came to her mother, Annie, she was not strong enough to accept them. Weroansquoa was sure this was the child she had waited for, the one to pass on the psychic gifts that had been given to her when she left the fires of the great shamans, long before Hatteras Island.

By the time Grandmom got back to the room she found a very different child. Ellie was sitting up in bed, her color was normal, and she was eating the bowl of soup Grandmom had left earlier.

"Grandmom, Weroansquoa just left." she said.

"I know," answered Odessa. "She said that you would be stronger now." The smile on Grandmom's face was one of relief. She knew her little girl would have a stronger life now. She knew this was coming but was a little anxious of how it would affect Ellie. Finally, the day of gifts had come and gone, and the child lived through it.

⋆ 5 ⋆

The Cave

Grandmom kept Ellie quiet and in her room for the rest of the weekend. She would have kept her home from school, but by Monday, Ellie was feeling her old self again, maybe even stronger. She had a bit of a different look. Her cheeks had color, her eyes were bright, and she seemed in a happy place. As Grandmom fixed her hair, she didn't even wince like usual. Getting tangles out of her bushy hair was hard to do without causing discomfort, to the point that sometimes Grandmom just piled it up on her head and just hid the tangles with ribbon.

"Grandmom, I don't mind if you pull at the tangles, I'm getting to be a big girl now, and don't want any more ribbons. Some of the girls have round things, curlers they call it, and then wear a scarf over their head, and, they wear it all day long. I don't want to be that girl either, I'm going to start doing my own hair, and, Grandmom, I like braids. Can you teach me how to do it, maybe after school today?" Ellie felt like she was growing up, and she knew this was going to take away from their special time together, but she compensated by giving her a huge hug. It was worth seeing her grandmother smile and then, as the hug continued, Odessa laughed out loud. It was wonderful that she and her granddaughter had such a connection. She knew teaching her how to make hair braids would take Ellie a little practice and that would be even more fun, as they would continue to spend more time together.

Ellie's new attitude was obvious to the boys also. She seemed so *in charge*, and they were glad to have her back in the fold. Anytime one of them was sick, or having trouble with school, or friends, it was a given there were two people who would be on hand to inject either fun or advice into the mix. The three were back! Good times ahead.

The good times were short lived, as the nighttime was interrupted by more sounds of war off the ocean. It wasn't that they were not used to it, it was still unsettling, and yet, their hearts did not rush like before; Grandpop had gotten into the routine of leaving his warm bed to help wherever he was needed. And, this new routine began to have a normal feel. It was as if there would always be bombing over the ocean. It was so steady, and predictable.

Grandpop did take the boys with him one night. He made good on Blake's birthday present promise, as he awakened them both and they all crawled into the truck together, headed to the station. However, it was on the pledge that they would be quiet and stay out of the way. Cap'n Charlie wished a million times that night that he had not obligated himself, but of course he had to honor his word, though he wondered what he must have been thinking to put the boys in this situation. Luke had been such a help before, and he wanted to do something special, but this was not the place for a little boy. Had he known what was ahead, he would never have made that particular commitment. He warned Luke that he had better clap his hand over Blake's mouth if he thought he was getting ready to talk. They all laughed about it, but the funniest part was when Cap'n Charlie picked up the other men, it seemed that no amount of conversation from the older men to Blake could make him talk. He just grinned. Charlie told them what the problem was, and everybody had a chuckle.

To the man, they all knew Charlie's youngest, and knew what a question box he could be.

When they got to the station, Blake grabbed Luke's hand and did not let go until he got back home early that morning. His eyes were so big at all that was going on. A huge merchant vessel had been hit, maybe three times, and it was sinking fast. The telescope was on it, and men were shouting out orders to the sailors in the station, as they prepared to go out to hopefully rescue the men. This time it was a tanker, which meant burning oil, and everybody was anxious. As the boys found a corner that had several vantage points, they watched as men loaded what they dared, in anticipation of the boat being filled with survivors, supplies took a back seat to room for human cargo.

When a person was burned, it was best not to touch them, damaged skin being so fragile, any handling simply tore into it more. They did carry a sling, which would help in getting men out of water into the boat. Also, it did not take up much space. They were hoping the oil had not yet spread so much that the men could not get out of it. Fire! Probably the most dangerous situation they could encounter. Men had to be strong enough to fill their lungs with air in order to stay under the solid sheets of fire on the water until they found a place to stick their head up and grab a breath. There was no other way of getting out of it. Many men drowned because they could not find that clear spot to fill their lungs with the air they so desperately needed.

When the boats left the station, the locals busied themselves preparing bed, salves, and listening to Dr. Folb about just how to treat burned victims until they got more help. Cap'n Charlie sent the kids to the tower to sit quietly, away from the business that was going on around them. He also did not want them to witness the victims, some would be dead, as he had not anticipated such a dramatic scene as this, with burned victims. The boys got to the top, and found another corner and sat motionless, just listening. They heard on the wireless that other boats were on their way to the scene. Timing was crucial, there was little hope for those who had to wait for a second boat to reach them, after leaving and having to come back for more. Those fishermen who had sea worthy vessels were also on their way. There was literally a flotilla of private boats going to the scene, with little thought of getting hit by a torpedo themselves.

Those brave men risking their lives to get to the stricken ship, were scared, but most felt like it was their son they were trying to save. This must have been happening on every shore plagued by the ugly German killing machines. The islanders in their small boats were hoping that on some foreign beach other communities were helping those whom they did not know. Even as they could hardly believe that this was happening to their island, they were proud to be shouldering the burden to keep others spared the sights, sounds and smells of war. They all had relatives and friends who were unaware of this feeling, and they were glad. When they reached the area of destruction, the civilians hung back and listened for instructions from anyone with a bullhorn. If they could hear anything, they followed directions, of not, they calculated the best way to help, and followed through.

They were not aware that the U-Boat had gotten what it wanted. It was not there to destroy men, it was there to sink ships, and when that was accomplished their job was done, their mission was on to finding another ship. Germany gave a prize for tonnage of ships sunk. Once they reached 100,000 tons of total destruction, they were honored in their own country with the Knight's Cross, Germany's highest honor of the war. In Germany, these killers were treated like movie stars, and complimented everywhere they went. Also, the U-Boats were only large enough to carry twenty torpedoes, and when that supply was exhausted, they had to return to their base in Europe for more. They were careful not to squander torpedoes before they reached the magic number for tonnage. Therefore, there would be no wasting of valuable munitions on a fishing boat, no matter how many lives it was carrying.

Sometimes, when there seemed to be no other prospects on the horizon, the U-Boat would hang around, and using deck guns, strafed the lifeboats with enough holes to sink it, while they watched as men struggled in the ocean. This was a case where there were so many private boats in the area that the Germans were not sure if any of them had guns, so they did not surface at the scene. Plus, from underwater, they could see through the periscope that the lifeboats were burning as soon as they hit the oil. The enemy was correct not to surface on this one, these were island men, and to the man, they had their rifles, and were just looking for a chance to pick off any figure they saw on the top of the deck of one of those monsters. These men had seen enough lifeboats on the shore riddled with holes to know what was taking place out at sea, and they were mad and ready to even the score if they could.

It was a long eventful night, and Cap'n Charlie wished more than a couple of times that he had not allowed the boys to come. But actually, he did not see them until the moment he and the others were ready to leave, and he went looking for them to go home. The ride home was quiet, nobody was in the mood to talk about anything they had seen. The boys were of the same mind, as they huddled together in the corner of the truck, and just closed their eyes against the memory. They were glad Pop had taken them, but they did not want to go again. These boys grew up a little bit more that night. This had been a week of growing up, for all three children. The boys decided not to tell Ellie what they had seen, and Ellie did not ask. She had concentrated so hard when she heard them leave with her Pop that she had actually *seen* what took place. She also *felt* what the boys felt, and was well aware of what war was all about upon *knowing* the things the boys were seeing.

Ellie wrapped her blanket around her and tiptoed into her grand-mother's room and crawled into bed with her. She snuggled up tight to the only mother she had ever known, and only then, touching her "mom", did she shut her eyes against all that her mind was seeing. Grandpop came to bed late, and tired, but seeing that little head next to Odessa, he smiled, and snuggled in beside them. He felt lucky to have this opportunity after what he had just witnessed. The next morning, Ellie awakened to an empty bed and the smell of breakfast downstairs. The world was normal again.

There was nothing to say about the events surrounding the night before. Everybody knew what happened and were in no mood to continue the thoughts of it the day after. The acrid smell of oil, smoke, and gunpowder coming from the sea permeated the air, making the islanders almost forget what a sweet smell the pure ocean breeze normally carried. They all tried to get back to the day ahead of them, the everyday activities that kept them alive. Death closed in on them and bothered their sleep. The fear of what was happening elsewhere where their men and boys were in harm's way, could not be any worse than this, if it was, they preferred to block it out of their minds.

At last the weekend was once again upon them, and the children could get out and move around. They rode their horses in the village and sometimes on wooded trails, just to give them exercise. They knew the horses wanted to get to the beach, but after seeing how much tar and muck had washed up they were not in the mood to be reminded. Ellie decided she would change the scenery.

"Since we can't go anywhere else, let's go down into the caves and explore. We haven't done that in a long time, and we are always talking about it. We are safe there, we can take the wolves, and they probably miss us, all except Blake's, Theo sleeps outside his window every night. What say? Want to?" She was almost pleading, she wanted to laugh again, to do silly things again. Being in the house with Grandmom and Aunt Nett brooding about the war was taking over their lives.

"Hey! I want to!" Blake's enthusiasm was exploding all over his grinning face.

"Yeh, sounds good to me," said Luke, "I'll get the torches ready, we only need a couple, cause remember we rewrapped the ones on sticks on the walls, and all we have to do is light them from one of ours, and do it each time we find one."

It was decided, the cave it was. They took the entrance from behind Uncle Jabez's fireplace in his office, hoping the grown-ups would be too tired, or lazy to come upstairs to look for them. They yelled down the stairs, "We're up here," and went about gathering up items they would need. They did not know exactly how to dress, so they dressed warmly and took along another jacket just in case. They all wore hats, especially Ellie needed assurance there would be no spiders down there. Weroansquoa said the wolves did not like them, and of course no snakes, they didn't like them either. But, it was too cold for crawly creatures to be moving around, the snakes were probably somewhere shedding their old skin.

Luke had never forgotten about the cave, he kept remembering that step back behind the waterfall when he was retrieving the chests. It was not a solid wall, there was another cavern behind the waterfall. He did not tell the others, Blake especially, since he thought it might prompt him to try to explore by himself. Or, worse yet, the little chap would hound him to death to get back down there. In his dreams, and in his subconscious, the cave loomed in his head and had to be pushed back. After all, that cave had been there as far back as the Croatoan, and must have been secret then, as Manteo had never mentioned it, nor taken him there. Even more puzzling, Powwaw had not said anything, and it was not a place the two ever went.

The more he thought about it, the stronger the urge became to give it another try. The thoughts and dreams would not go away, and as he became aware of items being discarded in the move from the lighthouse, he began to see some things that could help him in his quest to further explore. Wood could be a floor or the handle of a torch, depending on size and shape. Some of the objects were heavy pieces of sail, or cloth Grandpop was discarding that was formerly used to clean the lens of the

Fresnel light, that, if soaked in oil, would be sturdy enough to hold fire and not destruct.

He knew he could use it most of it, and after all, no one else wanted them, and they were throwing them away. He even saved old shoes from his grandfather or uncles, to wear, figuring if he used heavy socks, he could make up the size difference. They could also be left on the site for the next time. He even collected shoes from his mother and grandmother, for Ellie to use, making their visits less noticeable. Old brooms and boat paddles could be used for walking canes or prodding into unknown spaces. His far-a-way looks peaked Ellie's interest and without the lighthouse beam to help her fall asleep, she began to get into Luke's mind. It did not take long for the cave to appear, but, unlike Luke, she saw it all.

Ellie gave it away when she mentioned the cave and said, "Luke, did you ever figure out the tunnel behind the waterfall?"

"What did you say?" he gasped. He thought he had imagined that she spoke, maybe it was only in his head.

"I said, did you figure out the tunnel behind the waterfall?" Ellie tried to be casual, but knew at that moment she was going to have to confess to being nosy.

"Ellie?" He questioned.

"I've been thinking that something was bothering you, so I wanted to help. Luke, you might not like me for this, but I was so worried about you, I let myself enter your dreams. Honest Luke, I didn't really know I could, and maybe I shouldn't have, and I've never done anything like that before, and I won't again." The words were tumbling out of her so fast it was almost an unconscious confession that even surprised Ellie herself.

"I'm so sorry," she said to Luke's shocked silence. "But I thought it was something bad, and then when I found out what it was, I was so relieved. But I had to tell you what I had done, because I would just die if I thought you didn't trust me, so I had to tell. If you are mad or disappointed in me, just know it will never, ever, ever, happen again."

Luke took a long pause, and when he looked at Ellie again, he saw her almost in tears, but when she turned to look at him, to try to apologize again, she was relieved to see the kindness in his eyes and the relief on his face.

"It's okay. Ellie, I'm glad. I was going to tell you but there was so much in my mind, and my imagination was crazy since I was the only one to know there was more to the cave than we thought, plus I wanted to tell you first, so you could help me tell Blake. I didn't want him to get ahead of us, until we could both figure out what might be there. Maybe nothing." he paused.

"Oh yes Luke, there is something—that much I saw. If it had been nothing, I would not have bothered with it, but I saw a long cave, with several other openings going back as far as I could see, there was not much water, and I knew we could go back there. But, I didn't try to see too much."

"It's okay, I would have asked for you to try to vision it anyway. Boy, this is going to be fun. Now I know we will be safe, because you won't let anything strange happen to us, you will see danger before it happens." Luke was relieved. He felt like they were all bonding with the gifts they had been given. He was not threatened by Ellie's powers, he knew that combined with both he and Blake, they were actually stronger together, plus, here in the cave, they might need it. This was their first dangerous adventure together since Ellie was given all her gifts.

Once inside the cave, they lost no time getting to the waterfall, it was what was behind this that they wanted to explore. Knowing they were going behind the waterfall Luke and Blake had their sou'wester slickers, and Ellie found an old one belonging to Grandpop. Blake, as expected, was really excited when Luke handed him the yellow slicker and said where they were going. When they reached the falling water coming from the natural acquirer where the Indians got their sweet water, Blake went first. He knew from Luke that it was slippery, and he was careful to step hesitantly, feeling the slick rock beneath his foot, and trying not to slip.

Ellie was next, Blake helped her through and Luke, behind her, made sure she was safe. Within a few minutes they were all on the other side of the falls. It was beautiful in the firelight, with their shadows drifting down the cavern and splaying out on the walls. Somehow, the wolves were already there. Of course, they had a lair in one of the ante-caves.

They began to poke around the underground caverns of the Indian caves. They moved aside the roots hanging down from the trees above, so nobody would get scratched—the trees were dormant from the winter anyway. The Indians had secured the walls with a paste of crushed gravel and limestone from across the sound, and shells which had been finely ground. The shells glistened like diamonds as the torch light hit them, making the walls shimmer and shine.

Luke's idea of making torches and wrapping them in oil-soaked sail-cloth was working and putting the torch next to the cave walls revealed the protrusions the tribe left to hold the poles. They had placed torches on the walls in front of the waterfall, but this was a new area, and they were readying the area for the many visits to follow. He placed a home-made torch in each indentation he found. He had also taken the precaution to bring flashlights, so there was no reason to light the torches just now. This was just an experiment, and so far, a good one. No matter, they had light now. Every few feet, he and Blake gathered small pieces of wood from roots and pieces of trees they found scattered about and piled them in small stacks for firewood. They discussed bringing down more firewood, and kindling. Blake, who was never without his flints, would be able to light both the torches and the small fires for warmth.

The Indians had taken advantage of the subterranean stream as the cave stretched along with it. They made sure there were outlets between the solid walls for air to both come in and escape. Luke thought the Croatoans might have stayed here during times of suspected invasion, or storms. He kept a journal handy to make a map of where he thought the openings would reveal themselves above ground and planned to retrace his steps. He had learned from Uncle Jabez's journals to keep notes, and he knew he would be back. He planned to use the journal above ground, to possibly track what was below with what existed above. He needed to know the outlets, he knew if this was a hiding place, someone seeing smoke would give them away and so far, he had not figured out how to prevent that. He was anticipating the Germans coming ashore, and in his mind, his family would be prepared.

Even without finding anything, the adventure was exciting and the challenge to solve problems kept his mind sharp. The roof of the cave was maybe six feet high in most places, and higher in others. It must have taken the Croatoan years to create this hiding place. Luke reckoned it must have been as exciting for them to dig it out, and secure it, as it was going to be for him to enhance it. They could sometimes hear the action of water overhead, and he knew the passage ran either under the ocean or the sound. He also realized they were getting deeper than when they first started out. The floor was getting more moist as they went along. They began to be aware of the caves sloping downward, yet they were too curious not to continue. They passed several openings going both right and left and shined a light to see if they went deep, they all did. However, the kids did not stop to explore, they just kept going, not wanting to stray from their forward path, lest they get lost. There would be plenty of time to completely get familiar with this new underground village.

As they poked and prodded, Blake found something. "Luke, bring the flashlight over here. I found something the Indians left." He poked about with his stick and prodded with the toe of his shoe, and sure enough, there was something shiny there. With the light and all three kneeling down on the damp floor, they uncovered a shiny object.

"Look-e-here!" Blake shouted. "Pirate gold, I've found pirate gold!" He was so excited he started digging with his hands. He uncovered a small round object, about the size of a quarter. It was not flat but rounded on the top. Rubbing it with his finger, he uncovered something of gold, or brass, with an eagle engraved on the dome of the coin. It was not a coin, but a button. What would the Indians be doing with a button?

They all took a look at it and knew right away this was something they had to ask Grandpop about, but first, they would try to find out by looking in books. What was a button doing in an Indian cave? Maybe it was from a pirate, or just some kind of shirt or jacket worn by somebody. Who? They were puzzled.

"Let me see," said Ellie, and Blake handed her the button. Ellie felt a strange sensation, one she had not anticipated, and one that was not familiar. "I feel something," she said with a surprised look. She cupped her hand around the item and closed her eyes. Both boys had never seen that look and stared at her closely to see why she kept her eyes closed. Ellie's face changed, she still did not open her eyes, but just kept the button, now between both hands. Silence, from everybody. Luke and Blake looked at each other, and a smile crept across Luke's face. He knew.

Ellie spoke, still with her eyes closed. *This button is from a Yankee uniform. From the Civil War. It belonged to someone in our family. He hid out here for a long time. He had a brother who had food sent to him but did not come himself. The boy slept right here. He was a deserter, and he was afraid.* Ellie opened her eyes and looked at the shocked faces of her cousins. She acted like she had not spoken at all and seemed surprised at herself holding the button. "What's this?" she asked and looked at the boys for an answer.

Luke's grin was now full blown. "I knew it!" he said, "I knew it!" He grabbed Ellie by the shoulders and hugged her. "I knew it! Look at what you can do…just look what you can do. I knew when you put the other hand on top, you were going to feel what that button was all about. I knew it." He could not stop saying it. He was so excited, you would have thought they had found a bunch of pirate gold.

"Somebody tell me what is going on!" Blake demanded. "What are you two talking about? Gimme back my button, you guys are crazy." Blake reached out and a subdued Ellie handed him the button.

Finally gaining her composure, Ellie also *knew* it, and sheepishly looked at Luke. "I saw a young man, and he was sleeping right here. I saw almost his whole life right in my mind. I felt all tingly, and it came from that button. He was a Yankee soldier and he ran away, hiding in this cave. He was somebody who was connected to this family. I think he was a cousin, and he hid here because he had deserted the Union army. There were those who helped him hide, I think William's great grandson, whose name was, maybe Marcus, I can see his face, he was just a teenager. The owner of this button also had a brother, they were both sons of Soloman's daughter, who married a Jennette. I don't feel the brother, but he had something to do with the docks. He knew his brother deserted, to get away from the Yankees and he knew he came here."

Blake passed the button back to Ellie, now he was also curious and wanted Ellie to continue. Ellie took the button again, and the same feeling of "*knowing*" took over her, and she closed her eyes trying to *see* or concentrate on what the object was revealing. She paused, holding tight to the button, "*I know his name, it was Benjamin, and his brother was Thomas. Thomas was also a blockade runner and could not come get Benjamin, but a boy called Marcus, a free black boy, kept his whereabouts a secret, and brought him food down here. Marcus was the great-grandson of Uncle Jabez's friend, William who used to live here, and Marcus lived here also, and was best friends with the brothers. The Union army captured Benjamin and forced him into their army before he could get away. Benjamin was a not a Yankee, and did not want to shoot his neighbors, who were Confederates, so he ran away. This button was from his uniform. I'll bet if we go home and look in the encyclopedia, we will find this button.*"

When she finished, even she looked surprised. This was the first time anything like this had ever happened to her, and it was a little bit scary, but she knew it was exactly what Weroansquoa had told her would happen. It was just the first time.

"Ellie, look what you can do," Luke said. "I knew that was going to happen the minute Blake gave you the button. I just knew it."

At this point, the only one in the dark was Blake. "Somebody tell me what the heck just happened. When I'm holding this button, I don't feel a thing."

Now that Ellie had her wits about her she tried to explain what she herself was having a hard time understanding.

"Remember when I got sick just before you guys went with Grandpop to the station? Well, Weroansquoa visited me, and told me I was finally ready to get all the gifts the shamans wanted me to have. Weroansquoa's gifts. Receiving the gifts was what made me sick. There were strong feelings happening to my mind, and it was giving me a fever. Grandmom was afraid that maybe I would never get well, but after I slept for a while, I felt better. I knew something was different, but then everything felt fine. When you handed me that button, that funny feeling came back, and my inside mind went back in time to the button. I could see who was wearing it, a name came to my mind, and then I saw his life, the one he had while he was wearing the button. Because he was so close to his brother, I was also picking up his brother Thomas. I think I need to go home, and tonight, let's go to the attic, and let me hold the button again and see what happens. I don't know what happens when I hold it, I just know I see things. What do you think?"

Luke was the first to respond, Blake couldn't talk. He still looked confused. "Okay, I knew that would happen the minute I saw the look on your face when you touched the button. Ellie, I am so excited I can hardly breathe. You can see what happened in the past, when you touch something from the past. We knew you were going to be able to do strange things, we just didn't know what they would be. Now we know one of them. You know what that means?" Before any of the shocked faces could think of a word to say, Luke said, "we are all stronger together, we know that, we have tried things together when we only had little powers, now you have everything, so we have everything. Remember when you and Blake corralled the horses when they were in the sound at Mr. Burrus's ranch? It's that kind of thing. I think this time when you hold the button, we should all hold hands and see what the three of us can do. Let's get out of here, first, I'm hungry, and second, we need a better place to think. If it doesn't work, we'll come back down here and try it again. Okay?"

Luke had talked so long, Blake had recovered from his shock. He now knew exactly what was happening, and the button became more special to him. This was another thing he thought he would carry around with his flints. Pretty soon, his pants would be falling off, his pockets with all his treasures would be loading him down. "Boy! This is the most exciting day of my life," he said.

"Better than Spirit?" Luke knew the answer, but he just wanted to tease his little brother. It felt to them all like they were lighter, they just felt different. No explanation, just something had happened; they knew it, and they were going to prepare for it. If things didn't work in the house, they would come back, but everything in their lives just changed.

"I meant except the day of Spirit," Blake said, and he had the biggest smile ever.

The kids began gathering up the things they knew they needed to take back to the house and started the journey out of the cave. They could still hear water and knew that was something they had to look into, but this was enough excitement for one day, and they felt maybe Ellie needed a break. After all, it must have taken a lot of strength to get all that stuff out of her, and they didn't want her to be tired. She never had been the strongest, and with all this, they felt they better slow down. These strange things were going to keep on happening, and they better know how to respond.

Going back, they began to talk about the sound of water running, and what it could be. They could hardly wait for the next weekend to come around. This time they would be ready for it. Luke's mind was running so fast, he couldn't even talk, he had so many things rumbling around in his head. He was the leader, and he needed to take care of Blake, and especially Ellie. For a moment, he thought of what a lucky thing it was to be born into this family. He silently sent a "Thank You" to God, and to his guardian angel, Micah. He almost couldn't wait to get to church on Sunday. He had things to say.

The musty smell of the cave was replaced with a slight smell of oil, and smoke, accompanied with the reality of the life around them, and it was a quiet three children that sat down to the table that night to Grandmom's drum stew. This was one of the first drum fish to make the trip down the island. Drum was a specialty of the island, and when they were "running," there was not a fisherman on the island who was not on the point with a fishing rod trying to catch one. They were huge, and quite tasty. The islanders made a stew with potatoes, onion and special condiments. This one was early, and of course, Cap'n Bernice would be the one to catch the first one, maybe a month before the others showed up. He was truly the best fisherman on the island, maybe because since retiring from the Coast Guard, he fished every day. Grandpop did not fish, he had no time, so when his friend Bernice caught fish, he always shared. What a treat it was when he stood on the porch with the huge fish in a bucket. Grandmom got to cleaning and preparing it immediately.

Usually the children ate as much as any adult when this was in front of them, but tonight, they just picked at it, and after a while, asked to be excused from the table. Their mother and grandparents noticed the change and inquired about it.

"Tired," they said, "just tired."

DRUM STEW

3 lbs. drum fish, cut in chunks about 2 inches apiece
6-8 medium potatoes (diced in halves & quartered)
4 onions diced
½ lb.salt port, cut in small chunks
2 cups water

Boil drum and potatoes until potatoes are tender.
In small frying pan, fry salt pork and lightly fry onions, place
salt pork in pan with potatoes, add onions and meat.
 Add salt and pepper to taste.

HUSH PUPPIES

1 cup cornmeal
½ cup flour
1 tablespoon sugar
1 egg
1 teaspoon baking powder
½ cup milk or buttermilk
Pinch salt

Mix all ingredients together and drop by spoonful into hot
fat until golden. Dip spoon into water after each use.

Civil War

The children were tired, it had been a busy day, filled with more excitement than they had ever anticipated. Ellie was especially tired, even the boys noticed and, as the leader, bent on taking care of his younger brother and cousin, he suggested they go to bed and relax. There would be time enough for all they wanted to do on the days to come. That night, the U-Boats struck again. This time somewhere near the north shore and opposite Kinnakeet. It was so far away from their house on the hill in Trent Woods, they did not hear it, and Pop was able to get a good night's sleep.

The next morning, Sunday, everyone readied themselves for church. The huge church bell on the top of the Methodist church in Buxton sounded impressive as always, even though they could barely hear it, they anticipated the sound, and could always hear it from the top of the hill. The sound filled the community, and this morning, the church was especially full.

The men of the congregation gathered outside before church as usual, and it was then they heard of the latest German strike. It seemed, that more than one vessel was hit the night before and several stations responded, with the men from Kinnakeet and the northern tri-villages responding to the scene. It put a damper on all that was to be celebrated at the church. A solemn group of men entered the services, and though the groups split up by age, for the different Sunday school classes, the adult morning lessons took on a very serious tone.

The preacher came from his early morning address at Hatteras village, to the 11:00 am service at Buxton church. Of course he also had heard of the latest tragedy, and his message took on a reminder of hope. This particular Sunday, the children sat in one of the front pews with their mother and grandparents. It didn't seem proper to sit in the back with the other kids, and goof around. Luke and Blake especially, after what they had seen several nights ago, were reminded of the bodies of the wounded, and they didn't much feel like "church antics." At the end of the service, Rev. Sullivan asked Ward Barnett, if he didn't mind, on such short notice to come to the front and sing "The Lord's Prayer" as a benediction. Ward had the most magnificent baritone voice in the village, and of course he accepted. When he got to the front, he asked if it would be all right if Nett Finnegan accompanied him on the piano. They performed at local weddings together, and he was comfortable with the arrangement he knew she would play. The pianist gladly relinquished her seat for Nett.

Ward began, his voice boomed across the tiny church in the most beautiful baritone modulation, captivating the heavy hearts with hope. Luke moved first, with tears for his father, the men he saw from the burning ship, what might happen, all rolled up in that handsome young face, he reached down and grabbed Blake's hand, and they crawled over their grandparents to the edge of the pew. On the way, Blake gave his hand to Ellie, and the three holding hands moved toward the altar where Ward was standing. Ward was unaware, as his eyes were closed in prayer, but what happened next was quite remarkable. Cap'n Charlie stood up, as did Miss Odessa, and began to follow the children, but were blocked from getting to the isle by the people rising in front of him getting to their feet. At this point, everyone who could stand, did, and within a matter of minutes the whole church was kneeling at the altar in hopeful reverence for their loved ones in the war. The full church congregation wiped back tears, some were more vocal than others with their sobs, and the prayer lifted up that morning was typical of a community steeped in the belief that better days would come.

It was a teary eyed group of villagers who left the church that day, and if such a thing was possible, their hearts were lighter, and they all felt almost cleansed of the weight of worry for their loved ones, and of the hate for the enemy who was trying to destroy them. It was a day to remember, and a feeling that they all hoped would stay.

At home, the heaviness of the morning gave way to Grandmom singing hymns at the top of her lungs while frying chicken. Grandpop relaxed on the front porch, blew smoke rings, and just day dreamed, so proud of his brood he could not find the words.

That afternoon, company came, and Sunday began to look like Sunday again. The kids took the opportunity to go to Uncle Jabez's study and talk about how to help Ellie reconnect with Benjamin Jennette. Blake went to his stash of collectables on his dresser for the button, now in a prominent position between Mingin's carved wolf, dolphin figure and the new reddish horse carving given to him for his birthday by Ellie. Soon, if his collection grew, he would have to provide more space.

They quieted down, sat in the middle of the floor under the window which faced the sea, and held hands, each in deep concentration, hoping for a connection. Had they not had their eyes closed, and looked around, they would have seen that the room was cast in blue and silver shadows, and what they could not see was the figures of their saints, Micah, Travis and Brendan, also holding hands and approving of what they were watching. Saint Travis was proud of Ellie and sent affirmation to her for the trip back in time she would be taking in her mind.

It was not long before Benjamin, Thomas and their friend Marcus came through to all of them and began to reveal the horror of an enemy which forced them to fight against their neighbors. It seemed that he was not the only one coerced to fight for the Yankees. He did not know how many others deserted, but they were all plotting how to get away.

The pictures of the Civil War revealed to their minds were vivid, and the children were drawn into the story revealed by their distant relative, Ben Jennette.

According to Ben, Hatteras was again the focal point of the enemy in relation to getting into the back door of the South, the same as when in the Revolutionary War the English wanted to use the entryway for purposes of attacking more profitable cities inland. The tiny island was what stood between the Yankees and the path to Richmond, the capital of the Confederacy.

In 1846, a huge storm hit the coastline directly, and stayed around long enough to cut two very important inlets in the line of islands that were on the outer edge of North Carolina. One was just above Pea Island, between that area and the mainland. It was named Oregon Inlet, taken from the name of the first ship to successfully go through the new break in the land. The ship, a side wheeled vessel, had been thrown by the powerful waves of the hurricane over a sandbar, washing them from the sea into the Pamlico Sound. Here, it was stranded. Once the storm subsided, the crew, seeing themselves in shallow water and trapped, saw an opening not previously there, and as high tide arrived the water from the ocean rushed in, lifting the vessel enough for it to go back through the inlet to the ocean. Most thought the breach would fill in, as did others, but instead it widened.

The second important inlet was cut between the village of Hatteras and the island land mass of Ocracoke. This had happened before, but after the last storm the land filled the inlet, leaving the island connected again. Now, with the inlet opened again, it moved shipping from the inlet between Ocracoke and Portsmouth Islands to the new opening, larger and deeper than before, and right off the Hatteras docks.

The Hatteras inlet provided a battle plan for the Yankees. From this island, they could control whatever vessels sought to access the sea from the mainland, preventing North Carolina from shipping goods (Europe was still buying cotton) to foreign countries from the inland cities. It also made an entrance into the Pamlico Sound, thus once again giving a way to move troops into the major cities of the state with the rivers that rambled into the interior of North Carolina. Most of the larger cities of the state were located on one of these rivers, so, controlling Hatteras Island, became a must for the Union soldiers. The North was also interested in the new Oregon Inlet, which led to other interior cities of North Carolina through the Albemarle Sound, which also connected to several other rivers leading inland into North Carolina.

In 1861, North Carolina Governor, John Ellis, ordered all North Carolina lighthouses to extinguish their lights to keep from aiding the potential invasion by the North. The Cape Hatteras light was the most important and had recently been fitted with a new Fresnel lens. As states began to secede, they removed the lens rather than just going dark. As a result, the most important lens, the Fresnel lens, was taken from the Cape Hatteras Lighthouse. When the lens' were returned after the war to other lighthouses on the coast, the special one from the tallest brick lighthouse in the United States, was not to be found. For years following, the search was on for the missing lens from the Cape Hatteras lighthouse. As a result, after the war, the lighthouse was fitted with another lens. As the sentinel which bordered the Gulf Stream, and the dangerous Diamond Shoals twelve miles from shore, the necessity of a proper light to prevent ships wrecking on the shoals from either lack of knowledge, or storms, was paramount. The original lens was not recovered until 2002.

Hatteras Island was the first place occupied by the North. They ravaged the villages, took possession of needed houses and livestock, and within days captured the two forts at the mouth of the inlet, Forts Hatteras and Clark. These forts had been hastily erected and not properly fortified at the time, and therefore fell easily. At this point, the inlet was closed to trade with the mainland, and provisions were cut off. The Union basically forced the residents to pledge their allegiance to the army of the North. This happened so fast after the firing on Fort Sumpter in South Carolina, which set off the war, that the villagers had not even had time to think about whose side they were on, as they were only on their own side, figuring they might sit this one out.

As the first conquest by the North of the South, Hatteras was declared the capitol of the Union by the directive of a preacher from Virginia, assigned to the Hatteras Methodist Church, Rev. Marble Nash Taylor, and a staunch Unionist, who had also declared himself in charge. In spite of Taylor's directive, the state government seceded from the union, ignoring the dictate. With a thirty-mile gap between the island and the mainland, very little attention was paid to Rev. Taylor's proclamation. Meanwhile the Yankees used seven warships to bombard the island, and within days, the forts fell. This sudden show of force also caused the fort at Beacon Island near Ocracoke and the fort at Oregon inlet to abandon their posts, leaving the barrier islands vulnerable to the Union takeover, as they both were considered indefensible.

Within a short time, Charles Henry Foster, a co-conspirator with Taylor, hurried to Washington, in an attempt to be seated in the Congress of the United States. Lincoln refused to recognize either as any representative of the Federal government.

Hatteras Island was a contested area. As the South fought against the North, the people of the island, were caught in the middle, and just wanted to be left alone. The so called forts were hastily built barricades whose position was intended to keep northern ships from entering the harbor. They were poorly manned, and even more poorly fortified. The Union moved in to occupy the mouth of Hatteras Inlet. Even this met with difficulty, as storms and rough seas hindered the operation, and added days to the conquest. At last the crippled forts fell to Yankee hands.

With the Union occupation of Hatteras Island, all trade from the mainland was halted, creating a problem for the islanders who at this time were dependent on trade with other mainland cities. The occupation of the island was, for the North, a futile effort to gain entrance to the mainland, as northern vessels did not have the knowledge of how to navigate the unexpected shoals that made up the Pamlico Sound. They also were unable to stop Rebel blockade runners who could easily navigate this body of water, so familiar to them. The successful runs by the "pirates", as the North called them, were able to both frustrate the enemy and delight the southerners.

The Yankees were ill informed of the conditions they would face with this easy victory. The forts were useless in allowing ships in or preventing vessels from leaving. North Carolina blockade runners, knowledgeable about the shoals, allowed the South to continue to sell cotton to Europe, thus still making money for the cash strapped south.

The conditions on the island were intolerable for the Yankee soldiers. Their suits of wool were unbearable in the heat, and the mosquitoes and green flies pestered them constantly. In ransacking the villages, they found little of value. They stole as much cattle, sheep, goats and hogs as possible, only to have the islanders steal them back. They stole from the private gardens of islanders, leaving the villagers with little food.

Both Yankee officers who were responsible for taking the island left for the mainland as soon as possible, leaving command in disarray. Communication was a problem, and when the Rebels on the mainland were rumored to be on the move to take it back, there were too many leaders who thought they were in charge to make any headway for a defense. Confusion led to poor decisions.

Meanwhile, the Yankees commandeered local men to join in on the fight. This proved to be a mistake, as at each opportunity the locals resisted their invaders and helped the rebels in their attempt to regain the island. There was more fighting along this coastal strip of North Carolina than in all other sections of the state combined.

There were about one hundred slaves and half as many free Negroes on the island. As the freed men helped the south, the slaves, those who did not escape to find freedom elsewhere, simply stayed on the island and tried, as did other locals, to keep out of the way in order not to be forced to fight with the Northern armies.

The stakes were high, as whoever controlled Cape Hatteras controlled the entrance to the interior of the state and the rivers of Cape Fear, Neuse, Pasquotank, Roanoke, Tar and Chowan. This gave access to one third of the state. Also, whoever controlled these rivers controlled the coastal railway, and the surrounding bodies of water. The much needed inlet at Hatteras became an obstacle with its narrow and treacherous channels. In the beginning, the South underestimated the determination of the North to occupy the inlet and erected fragile forts of sand and dirt and loosely constructed barracks. Three broadsides by the Federal side wheeler, *Harriet Lane,* were enough for the south to raise the white flag of surrender. In all, only six hundred rebels defended four forts, two on Hatteras, one on Ocracoke, and one on Oregon Inlet. This poor decision was soon remedied as Jefferson Davis, President of the Confederacy, dispatched an old English trick of issuing "Letters of Marque" to southern vessels, making them privateers given permission to harass and pillaging Yankee vessels.

Benjamin's brother Thomas, a fishing captain, was one of the most talented "runners" having grown up around the docks all his life with his cousins, he was familiar with the shoals, and came and went through the inlet whenever he off-loaded the treasures captured from the Yankee ships he encountered. His and other vessels were allowed to contact, destroy and plunder, capturing enemy ships and supplying arms to the south, and keeping the spoils for himself and his friends. He would have made his ancestors proud, especially Jabez. The South was fortunate to have him torment the more professional and better funded Union Navy.

It was also recognized that the coast of North Carolina was the most dangerous stretch of shore in the whole of the Confederacy, because of the storms and the dangerous Diamond Shoals. On the day of the successful attack to take the forts at Hatteras, a storm whipped up and sank many of the small boats carrying infantry to the island from the Yankees ships offshore. The first introduction for those soldiers to Hatteras Island was to have to swim to shore. That should have been a sign to the invaders that this would not be as easy as it looked.

Some said the rebels were drunk on the day of the battle, and it was a fact that moral was low, ammunition limited, powder damp and the beaches were not patrolled. These blunders were recognized and corrected as the Rebels made a plan to regain control for the South. This, however, was not soon enough to help the starving villagers, whose supplies had been stolen, leaving them skinny, gaunt and displaying vacant stares knowing they were outmanned and without any defense from the ruthless enemy. Most of the men had been coerced into leaving their homes, and those left were at risk.

Many homes were taken over by the Union to house their officers, removing the locals who lived there and forcing them to enlist relatives to take them in. There was a concentrated effort to occupy the mansion on the hill in Trent Woods. Several attempts were made, only to be thwarted by what the interlopers called "a pack of wolves". This excuse was not acceptable to the officers, and they went back armed to fight off the aggressive animals. As each group returned with the information that the wolves were too many in number, some suggested the possibility that the animals lived inside the house. One proposition was made to burn the wooded area to finish off the wolves. After consideration, this was deemed not such a good idea, as it would take the entire Union garrison to control the fire, and in such a wooded area as where the house stood, burning would likely catch and burn the entire island.

Buxton woods was, at the time, the largest and most isolated piece of maritime forest remaining in North Carolina. Noted for a unique ecological feature; the huge freshwater sites supported the woods and freshwater swamps and swales. It sustained birds, fauna and flora. Most only in danger of fire by lightning strikes, as the locals were careful to maintain this treasure. The freshwater ponds and marshes, called sedges by natives, were surrounded by palmettos, holly and dogwood. It was also the home of a large aquifer, used by the Croatoans as the source of fresh water for Buxton, Frisco and Hatteras. Burning the woods would have destroyed the island, and it is admirable that those in charge recognized this, and so gave up on occupying the house in the middle of the woods.

It did not take long for the invaders to feel the wrath of the locals, and in attempting to control the blockade running, they realized this was not a finished deal. The Yankees sent a garrison of men down the island to insure the northern end would not be available for the Rebels to return from the across the Pamlico, on Roanoke Island, and retake Hatteras. The 9th New York, led by Colonel Hawkins began immediately confiscating arms from both Portsmouth and Ocracoke Islands, whose inhabitants ran away. He had intentions of wanting to attack Hatteras village, take over the land, destroy the lighthouse, steal the cattle, occupy the homes and set up larger camps. He was soon joined by the 20th Indiana regiment whose job was to occupy the northern villages with 600 men, then return to the lighthouse, killing all the life in between. He organized a tugboat, *The Fanny*, to follow with supplies to prop up his men in Chicamacomico.

Meanwhile, there was a large Confederate battalion at Roanoke Island, and just as the Yankees thought, their plan was to take back the island using the 3rd Georgia regiment. The Union had already experienced resistance from what they called *The Mosquito Fleet*, a group of rag tag vessels armed with cannon and small arms that seemed to be successful against the more organized Federal fleet. The Rebels were depending on these small vessels to stop Hawkins and prevent whatever destruction he had planned.

Several companies of the union army trekked the sandy roads from Hatteras to Chicamacomico, located across the sound from Roanoke Island, in anticipation of meeting and destroying the incoming Rebel army.

While in the villages making up Chicamacomico, Rodanthe being the largest, the enemy completely overran the locals and took whatever provisions the islanders had, leaving them to either starve or die of thirst. The commodity they denied the villagers was drinking water. The army confiscated all rain barrels, and when they too ran out of water, they counted on the supply tugboat, *The Fanny,* which had been sent by the Yankees to resupply both water and arms to prop up the 20th Indiana.

The army did not expect the supply ship so soon and thus failed to meet it. In this amount of time, the South's *Mosquito Fleet,* four small side-wheeled steamers, the *Winslow, Beaufort, Raleigh,* and *Ellie,* which comprised the North Carolina Navy attacked and captured the *Fanny,* confiscating the intended Northern supplies, not only water but guns and ammunition. The gun crews of these small southern vessels were actually infantry, the 3rd Georgia. The South was looking for prisoners but found supplies instead. They ran up the Confederate flag and claimed the vessel. Then, they attached a barge to the *Fanny* to offload the troops from the 3rd Georgia and the 7th North Carolina.

The *Mosquito Fleet* continued to move through the sound to Kinnakeet village carrying the 8th North Carolina to block the additional Northern infantry, called the *Hawkin's Zouaves,* (volunteer units with the New York group who wore outlandish uniforms prominently sporting red trousers) which were coming from the forts in Hatteras. The 8th North Carolina intended to surround the Yankees fleeing Chicamacomico. Meanwhile the *Mosquito Fleet* was supposed to land at the Barnes Mill at Big Kinnakeet. Those plans were foiled as the fleet also got caught up on the shoals of the Pamlico Sound.

With all this going on the residents of Chicamacomico were the victims of both armies and began to pack up their belongings and move south where they thought there was no fighting. They knew the army of the South was coming to take back the island but were afraid of the oath they had taken to the North and anticipated the retaliation they might receive from their rescuers. They were afraid they would be branded as traitors for giving in to the army from the North. In war, one makes the necessary decision to stay alive, and locals on the island had been forced to go along with their invaders to save their families. Thus, they tried to leave their village before the South arrived. They tore down their houses, made carts for their belongings, and started down the beach, south to Kinnakeet.

Meanwhile, the Yankees realizing their supplies were not coming, also began to move back down the beach headed to the forts at Hatteras. The retreating 20th Indiana, fled in the unforgiving Carolina sun, discarding their shoes to make better time, and suffering the scorching sands of the island. The Yankees, who were fully dressed in their wool uniforms, now severely suffered in the heat, and as the Rebels followed close behind, they found the discarded blue coats, shoes, and packs on the unrelenting sand as the island began to fight back in the only way it could.

Thus began the "Chicamacomico Races".

As the two armies chased down the sand dunes, the *Mosquito Fleet*, with orders to fire on the escaping Union army, (resulting in a cannonball imbedding itself in a house in Kinnakeet) got stuck in the low tide and shifting shoals of the Pamlico Sound, thus allowing the Yankees to pass right by them. The chase ended with the Yankees stopping at the Lighthouse, worn out from the hot sands and heavy equipment, until another unit from the Hatteras forts, the 9th New York came to the rescue bringing water and provisions.

The Rebels found the journey south, chasing Yankees, also had its problems, as Yankee ships, manned by another regiment from New York and stationed at Hatteras was sent by Hawkins to sail north to an off-shore position near where the Georgia infantry moved in pursuit of the struggling Indiana infantry. As the southerners chased the northern Indiana infantry, now bogged down in the sand, the ships began firing on them at will, causing the Georgia infantry to wade into the sound on the back side of the island to keep from getting shot. Tired from the chase, the southern unit from Georgia camped just north of Kinnakeet to rest and resume the fight, in anticipation of being joined by the infantry they anticipated were loaded on the ships in the sound waiting to meet them. Thinking that the Mosquito Fleet had been successful, they discovered on arrival that was not the case, and they were now alone in the fight, as they could see the ships a mile into the sound, inhibited by the same shoals plaguing the North. Realizing there would be no help, with both the Union army and navy closing in on them, they saw the futility of their mission to go up against so formidable foe. The next day the 3rd Georgia began their retreat back to the northern end of the island, hoping to be picked up by the beleaguered *Mosquito Fleet*, and taken across the sound to Roanoke Island to regroup and devise another plan.

Both armies ended up being exhausted, however, each claiming victory. The two forces had concentrated on victory for themselves, with no concern for the islanders. The northern army smarted from the loss and misery they had experienced, and they retaliated by vandalizing the island all the way back to the Hatteras Forts.

The tragedy was mostly for the residents who had uprooted their houses and lives to get out of the way of the two bungling armies. They left in such a hurry some even left their Bibles, as they loaded all they could take on make-shift carts.

The island did not recover until the war between the states ended, which also ended the island occupation. Natives began to work their way back to the prosperity they had enjoyed before the war.

The Chicamacomico Races were the most famous of the skirmishes of the two armies, one north and one south. The story of the residents involved was a separate issue. Many locals tried to find a way to get out of the way of the Union army, but were constantly surrounded by the enemy, with threats to kill them if caught deserting.

Benjamin explained who he was and his connection to the children. Sabra's son, Soloman, had a granddaughter, Mary, who married a distant cousin, Frank Jennette. Mary also had boys who came of age during the Civil War. One was captured, Benjamin, and the other, Thomas, was a blockade runner. Thomas Jennette, and his brother Benjamin were great grandsons of Soloman Austin, and both grew up on the docks in the family business. Soloman's children, all female, also married into other island families, Odens, Stowes, Gray, and Barnette. The docks and the Trent Woods mansion continued to be passed on to relatives.

Benjamin was the one who always took care of the mansion and was familiar with the wolves. He knew from his history they were somehow connected, and although he did not interact with them personally as his great, great grandmother had, he knew the stories. Knowing the enemy wanted the house, he was captured while trying to protect it, and forced into the Union army. When he discovered the officers were going to live there, he deserted and went into the caves to continue keeping watch over it. He was content to allow the wolves to take over.

Thomas, wary of the same thing, kept near the docks and used his skills as a sea captain to create havoc for the Yankees by destroying every vessel he found on the high seas. He and Ben were responsible, through their clandestine activities, to make sure the wolves were left alone to continue protecting their property. Thomas eventually had six children, Ben had four. The Jennette family prospered, keeping their land and eventually passing the shipping business to the Odens and Austin's, distant cousins. Over the years relatives always protected the mansion in Trent Woods, but lost sight of its history, until the house finally passed to Odessa. The history and secrets were safe as it was finally so old, people just figured it to be haunted. The wolves were the only occupants.

The children were aware that Ben did not die in the caves, he lived to an old age, as did his brother Thomas. One of Thomas's sons became a light keeper, and that also became a part of the Jennette family story. Grandmother had already told the children that four of their cousins, William, Jabez, Mary and Aquilla, gave a portion of family land to the government to build a new lighthouse. Being a family that had a history on the docks, and at sea, the importance of erecting a beacon to find their way home was paramount to this island family, connected by both blood and spirit to the other families on Cape Hatteras.

The children unclasped hands and smiled. They should have known that Ben did not die in the cave, because they did not find any bones. Just a button. Once again, they recognized the part their ancestors had played in the island's past. Their ancestors were always involved, and proudly so. They realized they were also related to others on the island who did not share the Jennette name. So far, the Austin's, Odens, Barnett's, and from Pop, the Grays and the Millers. No wonder everyone was so friendly, they shared a past, and now a future. Understanding the revelation by Benjamin, they recognized the important part their island played in all wars. Cape Hatteras prevailed as the first line of defense to protect the mainland against attack from the sea. Here again, the U-Boats needed to be stopped here. We stood guard.

HATTERAS

A poem by Joseph William Holden

The son of Governor WW Holden was born in Raleigh, NC in 1844. When he was 17, he enlisted in the Confederate Army, and was stationed on Roanoke Island. He was taken prisoner and remained in captivity for a year.

NOTE: The wind king of the north challenges the torrid god at Hatteras. Here is the meeting place of the cold winds of the North and the warm winds of the South. Ten vessels stood idly by when the contest began, which was fearful and typical of the severe storms on the coast. Nine of the vessels were sunk in this Golgotha of the Sea, where vessels have been wrecked since Sir Walter Raleigh's time, and where "scattered bones have lain and bleached for ages."

> The Wind King from the North came down,
> Nor stopped by river, mount or town,
> But like a boisterous god at play,
> Resistless bounded on his way.
> He shook the lake and tore the wood,
> And flapped his wings in merry mood,
> Nor furled them till he spied afar
> The white caps' flash on Hatteras bar,
> Where fierce Atlantic landward bowls
> O'er treacherous sands and hidden shoals.
>
> He paused, then wreathed his horn of cloud
> And blew defiance, long and loud,
> "Come up! Come up! thou torrid god,
> That rul'st the Southern sea—
> Ho! lightning-eyed and thunder-shod,
> Come here and wrestle here with me!
> As tosses thou the tangled cane
> I'll hurl thee o'er the boiling main!"
>
> The angry heavens hung dark and still
> Like Arctic light on Hecla's Hill;
> The mermaids sporting on the waves,
> Affrighted, fled to coral caves,
> The billow checked its curling crest,

And ocean stilled its heaving breast,
Reflected darkness weird and dread,
An inky plain the waters spread—

Amid the elemental lull,
When nature died and death lay dull,
As though itself were sleeping there—
Becalmed upon that dismal flood
Ten fated vessels idly stood,
And not a timber creaked!

Dim silence held each follow hull,
Save when some sailor in that night,
Oppressed with darkness and despair,
Some seaman, groping for the light,
Rose up and shrieked.
They cried like children, lost and lorn;
"Oh Lord, deliver while you may!
Sweet Jesus, drive this gloom away!
Forever fled, oh, lovely day!
I would that I were never born!"
For stoutest souls were terror-thrilled,
And warmest hearts with horror chilled.

"Come up! Come up! thou torrid god.
Thou lightning-eyed and thunder-shod,
Come wrestle here with me!"
'Twas heard ad answered: "Lo I come
From azure Caribee
To drive thee cowering to thy home
And melt its walls of frozen foam!"

From every isle and mountain del,
From plains of pathless chapparel,
He drew his lurid legions forth—
And sprang to meet the white-plumed North

Can mortal tongue in song convey
The fury of that fearful fray?
How ships were splintered at a blow—
Sails shivered into sheets of snow—
And seaman hurled to death below!
Two gods commingling, bolt and blast,
The huge waves on each other cast,
And bellowed o'er the raging waste;
Then sped, like harnessed steeds afar,
Amid the midnight din of war!

False Hatteras! When the cyclone came
Your waves leapt up with hoarse acclaim
And ran and wrecked yon argosy!
Fore'er nine sank! hat lone bulk stands
Embedded in thy yellow sands
An hundred hearts in death than stilled,
And yet its ribs, with corpses filled,
Are now caressed by thee!
Smile on, smile on thou watery hell,
And toss those skulls upon thy shore;
The sailor's widow knows thee well,
His children beg from door to door
And shiver while they strive to tell
How thou hast robbed the wretched poor!
Yon lipless skull shall speak for me,

This is Golgotha of the Sea!
And its keen hunger is the same
In winter's frost or summer's flame!
When life was young, adventure sweet,
I came with Walter Raleigh's fleet.
But here my scattered bones have lain
And bleached for ages by the main!
Though lonely once, strange folks have come,
Till peopled is my barren home,
Enough are here. Oh, heed my cry,
Ye white-winged strangers sailing by!
The bark that lingers on this wave,
Will find its smiling but a grave!

Then, tardy mariner, turn and flee
A myriad wreck are on the lea!
With swelling sail and sloping mast,
Accept kind Heaven's propitious blast!
Oh, ship, sail on! Oh, ship sail fast
Till thou, Golgotha's quick-sands past,
Hath gained the open sea at last.

Adventure

The children sat for a while, thinking about what they had just discovered, about the war, about themselves, and about their family. The light was fading, and it was beginning to get cold up there on the fourth floor.

"We just connected," Luke said calmly, "I thought we could, but I wasn't sure."

"We are a team, and I knew we could, 'cause Ellie and I could, remember Luke, you sent us a message from the horse, when you were out in the sound asking us to help you corral the other horses, and we did? That was a connection, and we didn't have to touch. Only Ellie and I were holding hands." Blake was so trusting, of course he would be confident; he had no fear.

But Blake was correct, they always had the power, they just hadn't needed it. Weroansquoa always said that the power would come when it was for good. Both boys looked at Ellie. She was a little pale, but she had put in all the work, and maybe it tired her out. They were still under the impression that she was not physically strong. Ellie knew better, she was conscious of the powerful energy force that had surged through her body as she talked to Weroansquoa. The thought made her sit up straight, as something strong washed over her and made her smile. She thought that maybe, it was all the intense energy that her mother could neither understand nor handle. The gifts were ready to be passed on, the time was set, but not for Annie, they were to be bestowed on the new baby. Talking to Grandmom over the years, and having questions answered by Weroansquoa, Ellie knew how weak her mother had grown over time, and all Annie wanted was to give life to the baby she carried. Ellie had never been as ill as her mother had been, could it be that the gifts belonged to her all along, and not her mother? There were so many things to think about, and it was all this confusion that the boys were seeing in her face.

"I'm not sick, if that's what you are thinking," she said to her cousins, I feel pretty good, I was just thinking about my mother. Mom said she was offered the powers and could not control it, but I think that momma was just weak from worry that she lost my father. I think the powers were mine no matter what. I might have just inherited the problem with my blood, for no reason," (Thinking also that maybe her special illness was what drew the wolves to her, since they were known to follow blood.) "Lots of people have problems with their health, maybe that was just me. If anything, Weroansquoa took the health problem away, and I got stronger." Ellie looked puzzled and stared at the dusk settling over the land. "Let's go downstairs, it should be suppertime, and maybe Grandmom yelled to us and we didn't hear. We better go. Blake, take the button, I think maybe we could try to hold it again, and learn more, or maybe not." At that she shrugged her shoulders in a questioning gesture, as the boys marveled at her composure.

"The button belonged to Benjamin, and I think we have to find out extra things from some other way, 'cause Benjamin only knew what he saw, and heard. That was probably not all of it. I'm going to check some of Pop's history books; they won't have anything about this island in them, but they will have the war, and maybe some of the things we can put together on our own." Luke was always the smartest one of the group and that made sense. They couldn't go around the island collecting things from the Civil War to hold. There had to be more ways to learn the adventures.

Blake took the button, and they all shook off their experience and started down the steps, only to hear Pop's voice,

"You young-uns better get down here now. Your grandmother has called you three times already, and one more time and we are going to eat without you, and you'll have to go to bed without any supper!"

At that, they rushed down the stairs, giggling and racing as usual, and practically slid into the dining room. Everybody was sitting there, with their plates full in front of them, just waiting. OOPS! They needed to be more careful.

"Sorry," they all said in chorus. "We got to reading and lost track of time. Guess we didn't hear you," said Luke, always the one to take the blame.

The weather was warming up, causing the island to experience a strong spring storm. It was welcomed, as villagers hoped it would inhibit the attacks. It did, but for only two days, then the same thunderous blasts started up again.

There was only one sub chaser in the ocean off the island, the USS Roper, out of Elizabeth City. The chances of it ever finding a sub in all that water were slim, but sometimes the kids could see it go by as it searched. The noise continued, it was either the sound of U-boats, or depth charges, but the ocean was in constant turmoil. The kids worried about their dolphins, so one afternoon, they took the horses to the beach, not really afraid, because the U-boats did not attack as much in the daytime. They seemed to have a pattern of striking at night like cowards. They were a bad dream, more than a bad dream; a bad reality.

The beach air was welcoming to the kids and the horses. They could see the wolves in the dunes, and they had brought company with them, Rook, the raven. He was flying all around and seemed to be playing with the wolves.

"Look!" Ellie said, "Rook has finally found Grandmom, I guess he was missing all those shiny things he used to steal from her at the lighthouse. His nest is probably empty, and he needed more stuff. Look at him with the wolves, he isn't afraid of them at all."

They did not know that the raven's best friends were the wolves. The wolf was the reason they could eat. They would lead the wolf to a target, the wolf would kill it and tear into it with his teeth to eat it, and the raven would show up after the wolves were finished tearing the victim in little pieces, just small enough for the raven to eat, leaving enough for him to take back to his nest. It was sort of a team effort. Sometimes they would see the raven fly out over the ocean, stay gone for a while and then come back. They wondered what he was seeing. Was he a spy? There was not much the raven did not know and his curiosity would eventually come in handy. In legend, the raven warded off death, which was why it appeared in all those drawings of Norse gods, and also pictured on their shields. They were protection against death and a source of power.

The problem facing the kids was keeping the horses out of the tar which had washed up on the beach, especially from the torpedoed tanker earlier in the month. U-boats were looking for tankers which when torpedoed spilled the oil meant for tanks and planes overseas, but the immediate result was the oil which spread across the innocent ocean. They did their best. What they wanted was for the horses to get in a good run, but it was so difficult reining both horse and rider this way or that. The horses did not fully understand. Finally, Blake just let Spirit shoot out straight, tar or no tar, this horse needed to stretch his legs. Seeing that, Pegasus was right behind him, with Luke's grin at the chase, plastered his lips against his teeth as they went flying down the beach. There was never a moment the challenge to win left either of the two boys, but this time, Ellie moved forward on Blue, and gave chase. The boys were shocked, this really was a more confidant Ellie.

Out at sea, peering through the periscope, the captain of the U-boat was laughing out loud. "Look at those kids run!" he said in his finest

German, and urged the officers nearby to each have a look. It was a slight change from the sweat, and foul smell of the cramped quarters and stale air of the sub. They were so enthralled, that after checking the horizon for ships they took the sub close to the surface, allowing the sailors to have a chance to go topside just to watch the kids play as they peered through the binoculars. The enemy was, just for a moment, not the behemoth it was paid to be, but just men and boys, whose own sons and brothers were still at home, and hopefully racing some horse in some pasture far across the ocean. It would only be a matter of hours before they returned to the killers which war had made them.

About that time, one of them said, "Wow! Do you see the size of those dogs? Even our shepherds are not that big, I wouldn't want to run into one of those." And in each one's mind, they knew they would, as the captain was already deciding which of these guys would try to go ashore for some supplies. It would be the ones with perfect English. At that point, some of the men began to fake using imperfect English, in order not to be picked. Being chewed up by a monstrous dog was not something one would relish.

"Look at those giants, they are faster than the horses, look at that white one. That looks like my grandfather's shepherd, and it appears to be the leader." While the Germans were marveling at the "dogs," the raven was marveling at them.

The fastest horse seemed to be Blue, who had come from behind to even up with the two boys. Luke and Blake looked at each other as Ellie flew by, and both grinned. Having Ellie win was the greatest feeling, nobody cared which one was faster at that point, they had finally been able to reward Ellie for all the things she did for them, and for the times she had been left behind. It was like "your ladyship, you just go on by." Ellie nudged Blue ahead, she did not turn to see of anyone was following and she cantered forward a little faster as she and Blue morphed into a full-on gallop on the hard sand of the beach.

The sound of Blue's hooves on the hard surface seemed to match the beating of her heart. Her hair unraveled from its ties and swept back as the breeze washed her face with the fresh smell of salt and pure air. She felt like she was flying, and at the same time, she held on tightly to the reins, keeping her knees in contact with the horse's heavily pulsating midriff. She felt as though this was as close to true happiness as she had ever been. The thunder of pounding hoofs filled her head and she was totally unaware of anything or anyone at that glorious moment.

Behind her, Blake on Spirit, and Luke astride Gus, looked at each other in total shock. "Don't run those horses on the beach," Grandpop had said, "they are not old enough and their bones are not developed enough to handle the uncertainty of the sand." Ellie never before had disobeyed her beloved Pop, but this was right to do, at this moment, for both horse and rider. Ellie and Blue continued to create distance as she raced ahead. Both boys, without a word, nudged their steeds ahead, first not so fast, then looking aside to each other. They grinned as they went from a trot to a gallop, and each knew the race was on! Both leaned forward and tightened their grip as the horses jockeyed for position.

Ellie heard them coming and began to hold back on Blue to let them catch up. Spirit and Gus cast an eye toward each other and seemed to be in the contest of their young lives, almost unaware of the riders fastened to their backs, as they enjoyed the long stretch of their legs. They had never been allowed to go faster than a trot, and the need for a full on run was long overdue. The boys were now almost lying flat on the backs of their pets, with the long manes of both horses flying against their cheeks.

As they caught Ellie they did not stop.

"STOP! STOP!" Ellie cried out, "I waited for YOU!"

Both boys pulled on their energetic rides to a slow gallop, then a trot, as they turned around and headed toward their cousin. Each were breathing deeply, not in exhaustion but excitement. "Before they could even speak, Ellie blurted out, "I know that Grandpop said not to run them on the beach, but Blue just took off, and he was having so much fun, I had to let him go."

This was just the best afternoon ever, but, they would live to regret it, as cleaning the tar from the horse's hooves would be a chore they would rethink before they ever did it again. But for now, everybody was forgetting the war and just having fun.

All the fun stopped when the kids spied an overturned lifeboat, full of bullet holes, and several yards away, the bodies of two young men face down on the sand, too still to be alive. The children stopped cold. Pegasus walked near, and Luke warned the others to stay back. They wheeled their horses around and with their new found speed, and a new purpose, the kids raced back to the house to tell Grandpop. Equally concerned he rang up the Coast Guard, then with as quick a step, he hurried out the door. The war was once again a reality.

Solemnly, the kids returned the horses to the barn and began the chore of getting the tar off their hooves. Grandmom came to the barn with a plate of cookies and a carrot for each horse, also, a couple of carrots for the huge Morgan horses of Grandpop's. There was absolutely no reason to allow the war to take over their lives. In her own way, Odessa fought the Germans herself. This was ruining her family, because, if her boys were here, and Bill, they would also be eating comfort food. She felt adamant there was no reason to give in.

That week in school, both boys were on the hunt through some of the history books lying around, to find out as much as they could about the Civil War. When Luke asked Mr. Hathaway for a history book, he thought he saw him smile. Poor Mr. Hathaway, the Beal boy was driving him crazy. If the old man could, he would quit, but there was nobody to take his place, so if he just waited a few more months, this horrible school duty, on "a beautiful island" would end, and he would get back to a place where they wore shoes. But, Luke was thinking, I wonder if Pop has an old suit Mr. Hathaway could wear, unless maybe he likes the way he smells. Luke thought maybe he should have looked for a book in some other room, cause standing this close was as near a punishment as anyone could stomach. School, it had its drawbacks.

Both Luke and Blake had gotten hold of a couple of old history books and began looking through them. They learned that it was not just the island that had a hard time during the war between the North and South, most of the South dealt with the same things the island did, except they had their homes and crops burned to the ground when the Yankees came through. And, instead of hiding in a cave while the enemy searched, some young boys were gathered up and sent to horrible prison camps to be beaten and starved by the Yankee guards. War made human men inhuman in their actions. It was the same as now. Those men in the U-boats, maybe were just regular men in their own country. War had turned them into cold blooded killers.

While looking through his history book, Luke gasped, and went running into Blake's room. "Look! I saw this very ship when Willie and I went to see the ships resting on the bottom of Diamond Shoals. See that shape, with that round top? It says it was the first ironclad ship, and it was called the USS Monitor. It was sunk in a storm off here and went down at Diamond Shoals. Boy, that one is famous." As he talked Blake began thumbing through his pages, and eventually found the same picture in his history book. They wondered aloud how many ships would be on the bottom of the Diamonds now, with all this going on. "Looks like this island is a graveyard for ships, some from storms, and some from U-boats. I'm going back with Willie for another look when this is over." He paused, and in a small voice, to nobody in particular he said, "I hope Willie comes out all right." Both boys had a weak feeling wash over them.

"Maybe we're not the only ones, Luke," said Blake. "I guess all young boys see things like this when they go through war."

"And some boys, like Benjamin, are older, and have a harder time than we do. All we are doing is watching. I sort of feel lucky, but Daddy is fighting just like Benjamin, so I guess he is taking our place in the war. I wish he would come home." Sadly, Luke had a huge lump in his throat that he had to hide from Blake, but it didn't matter, tears were streaming down Blake's cheeks anyway, and they both moved closer, and rested on each other for comfort.

That night, Blake couldn't sleep, and he went to his window and looked out at his sleeping wolf. Theo always took his place on the roof just under Blake's bedroom window. Blake lifted the window quietly, and rubbed his wolf, then, he did something he had not planned on. He crawled out the window and sat on the roof with the huge gray "dog". Suddenly, the house shook, and Blake crawled to the edge of the porch roof to look out to sea. He was not in a position to see what happened, so he carefully went to the huge live oak tree and crawled over to grab onto the big limb.

By this time, Theo was also near the tree, but not on it, his path to the porch roof was one with several leaps from the chicken coop to the roof of the kitchen, then to the higher roof of the main house. Blake could see the fire coming up from the ocean, almost too close to the beach, this ship had hugged the shore to avoid being hit, but the U-boat had followed, and made a direct hit. The ship was burning, but still moving. What he could not know was the sub was on a shoal beyond the breakers and dead in the water. It had miscalculated what they were seeing on their depth scanner and had gone too far to shore and was stuck on an underwater ridge. They were unfamiliar with the random sand bars which cropped up all the time.

Blake saw his grandfather come out of the house and get into the old jalopy and head down the road which led to the village. He scrunched down on the roof to keep his grandfather from seeing him, and then, the thought hit him. I'm going to go see. It was chilly, and not wanting to go back to bed, he crawled back through the window and put on a coat over his pajamas. He was not aware the sub was still around, he could only see the fire from the ship. When Blake moved to climb down the tree, Theo went for the chicken coop, and soon they were both standing on the ground at the corner of the house. The two stood there for a minute, and Blake decided it would be quicker if he went on Spirit, and the horse being so dark, nobody would see them. He was about to have himself an adventure.

He led Spirit quietly out of the barn, Theo was nowhere to be seen, so Blake walked Spirit into the trees leading to the ocean and mounted him for the jaunt to the beach. As soon as he cleared the trees and headed over the dunes, he saw a small row boat, pulled up on the beach just down the way, south of the house. He could see the dark shadows of three figures slumped over a hole they were digging. He watched as they lifted the box lying on the sand behind them and dropped it in the hole. They began to fill the hole to hide the box. Blake could recognize danger when he saw it and attempted to rein Spirit around.

Before he could complete the turn, one of the men was standing in front of him, holding something. He reached up and grabbed Blake's foot and drug him off the back of the horse, causing the youngster to almost break his arm. Then the man dropped his possession in order to free his other hand, and with that, he gave Spirit a swat on the rump which sent him running. This guy must not have known much about horses, because Spirit took off running toward the barn.

Spirit was moving fast, sensing something was wrong, and as he reached the house, he began to whiney, and kept it up, until Luke awakened. Luke hurriedly hit the floor and first banged on Blake's door, then Ellie's, waking both Grandmom and Nett. He and Ellie raced down the stairs in their night clothes out the kitchen door to the barn. There they encountered an excited red horse, prancing around in a circle, and bucking like he was stamping out a fire.

They realized then that Blake was not with them, and putting it all together, no Blake, and Spirit in a panic, Luke ran back into the house and shouted up the stairs to his mother, "Blake's gone, he's in trouble, or Spirit would not be acting like this. I'm going to look for him."

"Me too!" shouted Ellie.

"Get back here!" Nett was also seeing trouble, big trouble, "get back here and put some clothes and shoes on. I'll call Grandpop, but you two get dressed quickly, take the horses and go." She raced back to the house, and Odessa was there with her hands over her mouth.

"Please hurry!" Grandmom said as she was fighting back tears. "What in the world is that child doing out on a night like this. What was he thinking?"

Both kids dressed quickly, and raced out to the barn for their horses, they did not bother with saddle or blanket, just the reins, and off they went toward the beach. In the woods, running behind them were the two wolves.

The Germans, dressed like fishermen, dropped what they were holding, and gathered the boy from the sand. It took two of them to hold him and cover his mouth to muffle the screams coming from the squirming boy dressed in his night clothes.

This was what Luke and Ellie saw as they dismounted and crouched down in the sand peering over a high dune. Luke looped the reins of both horses on a sea oat and inched his way next to Ellie. They both silently moved down the dunes to be opposite Blake, who was making a gallant attempt to free himself of his captors. The "fishermen" began to move the boat back to the water. *They are going to take him with them*, Luke thought. As he and Ellie tried to figure out how to overcome the three men, Luke started to get from his knees to stand and run for Blake, figuring the men would get confused if they had to deal with another kid, this one just a little bit bigger, and in Luke's mind, ten times madder.

Before he could rise, something large and dark sailed over his head, the wind from which caused the hair on the top of his head to blow. Theo, in one great leap cleared both Luke and Ellie, hit the top of the sand dunes, and in two strong leaps ended up in front of the man holding his master. Head down, teeth barred, nose wrinkled up to show the full set of sharp white fangs, a deep nasty growl cut through the night as he moved in a low crouching motion toward his buddy and the man holding him.

One of the men reached into his back knapsack and pulled out something black. Theo, in one more dexterous leap, snapped the arm of the man pulling the pistol. He began shaking the arm violently, back and forth, biting even harder at each attempt to break bone. At that moment Rafe, black as night, joined Theo, and moving fast, began to take on the other two. Growling and looking to be smiling, the white wolf, Twylah, whom the men had observed from the sub, just crawled across the sand in a crouch, and buckled one of the intruders at the knees, and with the man on the ground, she went for the throat. Above them was a raven, the watcher, who had summoned the other two wolves to help. In the dark of night, the black bird was circling the scene, ready to warn if reinforcements came. He was keeping the wolves on task.

Everything was happening so fast, the struggling Blake wrenched himself free, and ran to the dunes where both Luke and Ellie had shown themselves in an attempt to rescue him. Meanwhile, the mixture of screams and growls were vicious as Theo, having done maximum damage to the man with the gun, began to attack all three saboteurs almost at the same time. So intent on damage, he was unaware that the he had been joined by two other wolves, who were also tearing into the men. The scene was a ball of sand, blood and fur, with man and wolf indistinguishable from each other. As the men struggled to get away from the huge grey and his pack, the first man was bleeding profusely into the white sand, and the others, in their efforts to survive, were using their packs and possessions in order to protect their faces.

All of this commotion did not escape the two surfmen whose job it was to patrol the beach looking for survivors or boats from the stricken ship. They had mistaken the cries from the men to be cries from the victims of the ship, now seriously on fire and in danger of sinking. The closer they got, seeing the small boat, and commotion, they went in a full gallop to get to the scene. When they finally arrived at the darkened spectacle, they saw three "fishermen" showing deep cuts, torn clothing and bleeding, one writhing in pain on the ground, holding his obviously broken and blood-soaked twisted arm, with three children standing about twenty feet away, their hands over their mouths in a silent scream.

"What's going on here?" Bert, the older of the two surfmen said in a sharp loud voice. as he dismounted and walked up to the disheveled man flailing trying to fight off the huge monster who was determined to break him apart. It was so dark, the surfman could not tell what was happening, he heard the growl mixed with screams but could not distinguish the figures. There seemed to be a fight of some kind, as there were three men, obviously in trouble. As the surfman approached, the wolves disappeared into the dunes, leaving the bleeding man doubled over in pain, and the other two struggling in the sand, bleeding.

One of the "fishermen" shouted "MONSTROS …MONSTROS!"

The other shouted "WULF!" The third man in the sand was too injured to make sense.

At the same time, little Blake had found his voice and was yelling about a gun, and a box, and pointing behind the melee.

The second surfmen, Tolson, now standing beside his partner, leaned down and picked up a black object in the sand, and another not too far away.

Before that, neither surfman thought to call for help, as these men were in no condition to give them any trouble.

"Well," he says, "lookee what I found!", and held up two German Luger pistols, one dangling from each hand.

"Here's your wolf," he said.

"NO! NO!" the men protested, and in their broken English, mixing both languages together, "there was a wolf, then three … big as bears … LOOK AT ME … LOOK AT US! We are bleeding … we need a doctor!" they were beside themselves, shaking in terror, pleading with the two islanders, talking all over themselves, forgetting their "perfect" English and yelling in two languages at the same time. There was so much confusion, with the two trying to talk, motioning to the man on the sand bleeding out in the moonlight, holding their ragged clothes, and bleeding from several bites. The island men began to separate the parties and one by one they tied up the Germans, securing them to their horses.

"Wolf!" They kept saying over and over. In the dark their eyes shone wide and their faces were twitching. They were almost glad to have been "rescued".

As the local men were discounting all the yelling about wolves, Blake started to step forward to tell what was happening. Luke grabbed his head and hugged it to his chest, in an attempt to muffle his brother's yelling as the surfmen tried to get to the bottom of the story. From the looks of the rowboat, and the ill-fated attempt to pass as fishermen, along with the unskilled attempt at English, they knew their captives were from the sub that just fired on the ship off shore.

The moon revealed in the distance, a protrusion from the water as the breakers rose and fell to partially reveal the periscope of the sub waiting just beyond, too stuck to move, hoping their hiding place would not be revealed by the rising and falling of the surf. However, it had been revealed. The surfmen corralled the two suspects, rolled over the one on the ground, still breathing, and spilling blood all over the sand. Using their radios, they relayed their position for assistance. This night, with a stricken ship in the area, there were many men who would respond. All the while, the islanders were holding the German Lugers on the two and keeping watch over the severely injured man on the ground. Still the Germans were shouting in broken German/English about a wolf. The island men found it quite unintelligible.

The surfmen were not concerned with a wolf, they had just captured three German sailors who were attempting to get into the village. They almost forgot about the kids, the prisoners were so important.

There was no wolf.

When the kids were confronted, as they were also filling the air with chatter, they seem not to know anything about a wolf. They were not about to betray their saviors.

The surfmen were prepared, it was their job. They hastily tied up the three injured men, and left them wallowing on the sand, scared, bleeding and jabbering on and on about a wolf.

As everyone waited, the surfmen realized who they had, the pistols betrayed them, and lapsing into and out of the German language was of course a give-away. The wounded man bleeding out on the sand was in total German language now, as Tolson was trying not to alarm the sub which he felt was still in the area. He knew the enemy could not see what had happened in the dark, but surely, they must suspect. Other stations were on their way to respond.

Meanwhile, ol' man Tolson was questioning the children about what they saw. Of course, he knew they were Cap'n Charlie's grandchildren, so he believed their story of a buried box. Knowing that the box, if it existed, was going nowhere, he was calming the children down, and holding on to his prisoners at the same time, wishing help would arrive soon. He was still worried about the sub so close to them, and afraid they will be shot down on the beach, here, alone, with three kids. He radioed the station to notify the USS Roper of a suspected sub in the area, and hoping it was close enough to respond they also waited for other vessels from the Coast Guard stations to appear, and possibly block any exit the sub would attempt. He then requested a relay of the matter to the stricken ship. He was hoping it could move out of the way, he could not yet tell if it was completely destroyed, as all they could see was fire and smoke.

The USS Roper already knew there was a sub in the area because the torpedoed ship had transmitted a SOS upon being struck. The USS Roper began to track the calls to get an exact location, knowing they were within striking distance, but also unaware of the precarious position the in which the sub found itself, as it had misjudged the depth of the ocean floor in trying to sink the ship. The ship had traveled closer to shore than usual, and the sub had finally made a mistake, finding itself on an uncharted sand bar.

The sky darkened as Travis appeared in the clouds that moved through the partially lit moon. She was checking on Ellie, and quite pleased with her wolf's performance. All the Saints joined her as Twylah and Theo waited beyond the dunes, unseen by anyone. Rafe was so dark, he could almost blend in with the black treacherous night.

The stranded sub waited on the sand bar unable to flee, waiting for the tide to free them of their position. Their only visible indication was a bit of the periscope that showed slightly as a forming breaker revealed it. And, if anyone had looked to the sea, they would have seen a black object flying directly over a portion of the ocean. The object was circling something. The commander of the sub discussed at least getting up far enough to use the deck guns, and the possibility of mowing down the lot, but they could not move until the tide changed.

Now the scene began to fill up. There were other men with guns at the spectacle on the beach. Discovery would mean the end of their mission should they be captured, which, if they made a move toward the spectacle on the beach, would surely happen. They could also hear the engines of approaching boats. They were aware from sounds picked up on their instruments that there was also a larger vessel coming to the scene. They realized they were going to have to fight their way out of this predicament.

The Coast Guard cruisers arrived, one from Hatteras, and another from the station at the lighthouse. They kept traveling back and forth, between the suspected sub sighting and the sea, in hopes of keeping it there until the USS Roper arrived on the scene. The Coast Guard vessels did not have the equipment to fight off a sub, but they could certainly detain it where it was. It would be hours until the tide changed, so there was no hope of the U-boat escaping on its own. The military men on horseback waiting on the shore, secured the intruders, plus dug up the box Blake had seen them bury. It was full of explosives, grenades and ammunition for the guns they carried. By now, there were about fifteen men on the shore from the several stations, and they gathered up their captives, and the box of explosives, and headed to Creeds Hill Station in Frisco. Meanwhile the cutters, continued their movement to keep the sub in position until the *USS Roper* arrived.

Cap'n Charlie arrived on the scene to collect his kids. Surprisingly he was on ol' Tony, with Spirit in tow. He gathered up his brood, put Blake back on Spirit, and the four horses disappeared into the woods next to the dunes, heading toward home. The kids, at least Luke, sort of wished they could stay to watch the finish, but he was absolutely sure that was not going to happen. Charlie Gray showed no emotion as he gathered up his children, so they were not sure what kind of mood they would find when they got home. Quietly, they followed. The wolves, unseen in the bushes, kept track of the group as they all went back to the house.

When they arrived home, Grandmom and Nett were at the kitchen stoop, tired from worry and crying, to give all of them a big hug. They were not aware of just exactly what happened as the children seemed so stiff. The Captain gathered them all in the living room and lit the fireplace. Everybody was shivering, from cold or nerves.

In a very short explanation, the Captain told what he knew of the situation, and the involvement of the kids. "The two older women sat wide-eyed at what they were hearing.

He said to Nett, "Go get your hairbrush."

"No-o-o," said Nett, "Pop don't," she begged. "He's sorry, I can see it!" But her pleading fell on deaf ears, and she finally went to her room for the dreaded hairbrush.

"Charlie, is this necessary?" Grandmom chimed in.

"Definitely! And I don't want to hear another word about it!"

The three kids stood, as Nett returned, and walked toward their grandfather.

"No, you two stay where you are," he motioned to Luke and Ellie. "Blake, you come with me."

"Oh, Pop!" Luke burst into tears as he tried to block Blake from moving forward. "Choose me," he pleaded. "It will teach him a better lesson."

Captain Charlie motioned for Blake to follow him. "I don't appreciate your interference," he said to Luke, and from the scowl on his face, Luke stood back.

"Follow me, young man," and Captain Charlie walked to his study under the stairs. Blake followed, and his grandfather shut the door behind him. Once behind the closed door, hearing the muffled cries from the other side, his Pop sat down in the big chair he used when he took a nap. "Get across my lap," and he motioned the position Blake should take. A tearful Blake did as his grandfather said. Charlie raised the hairbrush and gave Blake a strong smack across his bottom. It hurt, no doubt about it, and Blake let out a yell. When he quit sniffling, Charlie raised his hand again, and this time Blake was ready. On the sound of the especially loud smack, Blake let out another yell. Then, he looked up in surprise as he realized his Pop had hit the chair, not him. With a surprised look on his face, he turned his head to see the tears in his grandfather's face. He raised the brush one more time, and Blake steadied himself, only to hear the blow but not feel it.

Charlie Gray reached down and set his grandson right, pulled him to a sitting position on his lap, and held him to his chest, sobbing uncontrollably. Blake put his arms around his Pop, and they both sobbed.

"Pop," he blubbered, through snot and tears mixed as they ran down his face, "I'll never do anything like that again, I love you so much, please don't hate me. Maybe I made you look stupid to your friends, and I didn't mean to scare anybody, Please, Please, I'm sorry!" all the while wiping his face, but he could not let go of his grandfather's neck. Poor Grandpop, his shirt collar was wet from Blake's happiness and pain all mixed in together.

"Son, I hope you have learned a lesson, and one more thing, here Pop laughed in his tears, "don't you EVER tell what happened in this room!"

With that, Cap'n Charlie pulled out a handkerchief and cleaned up his precious grandson's face.

Underground Buxton

"If you talk to the animal it will talk with you
And you will know each other.
If you do not talk to them, you will not know them,
And what you do not know
You will fear, and what one fears
One Destroys"

CHIEF DAN GEORGE

Captain Charlie came from his study followed by Blake, red-eyed and still rubbing his sore butt. Odessa and Nett made a gesture to rise from their chairs, but Charlie motioned for them to stay where they were. Luke and Ellie, also red-eyed saw the gesture to stay, and did not test it.

"What do you have to say for yourself son?" asked the Captain.

"I'm sorry I caused so much trouble, I knew better, I was just curious." Blake choked up on his words and kept his eyes on his grandfather's face. "Pop didn't tell me to say anything, that is just how I feel," he finished.

Before he could say another word, the sound of depth charges exploding in the ocean made everyone look up, then at each other. Ellie clapped one hand over her mouth and sent the other one to cover her heart. The room was silent.

"Caught yourself a U-boat, son." At that Pop flashed a grin and ruffled his grandson's head.

Blake looked shocked, still looking at his grandfather's face, he wrapped his arms around his Pop's legs and hugged on tight. Cap'n Charlie leaned down and said, "one more thing, I think you should stay in the house for a week, I need to teach you a lesson."

Blake reached up, pulled his grandfather to him and gave him a kiss, then literally ran out of the room and up the stairs. It was time for everyone to go back to bed anyway. Poor Cap'n Charlie, he got on his coat, and headed to the station one more time. There had been a truce called in the Gray household, but the war continued heating up on the ocean. Everybody gave hugs all around, and slowly mounted the steps to their various rooms. This had been a long day and night; they were all tired physically and emotionally. When the house was once again quiet, Luke pushed open the bookcase leading to Blake's room, only to see Ellie coming out of the closet she shared with Blake. Both of them quietly crawled into the bed with Blake, one on each side.

That was the way Nett found them a couple of hours later when she went to awaken them for school. She smiled, and tiptoed downstairs to the kitchen, Grandmom needed to come up and have a look before they coaxed them from their beds. Hearts went from heavy to light in an instant. Odessa and Nett thought they wouldn't tell Charlie because Blake was being punished, but they should have known he would have smiled. Which is exactly what he did when they were standing at the door of Blake's room looking at the scene and felt his presence behind them. It had been a long night, and Charlie had come home to get ready for school also. Grandmom noticed how hollow Charlie's eyes looked. He was sleep deprived, and probably wishing he could crawl into bed with the kids. She wondered how long he could go on like this.

While Blake was delegated to the house for punishment every day after school, he was so good at coming straight into the house and offering to help his grandmother with chores, some she saved so they could do things together. Grandmom made him his favorite snack, blackberry preserves and biscuits. He returned the favor by helping her wash clothes, she did the most scrubbing on an old corrugated metal wash board which was placed inside a galvanized tub. This was the same tub Blake had taken many a bath in, on the back porch over at the lighthouse. Sometimes the clothes were so filthy, since there was only sand, and no pavement, it made everything especially dirty. Grandmom soaked them overnight in Octagon soap. Blake helped her by squeezing out the clothes just before she hung them on the line.

She then ironed next to the kitchen fireplace, with big heavy iron pieces, about 3"x5", flat on the bottom with a rounded handle on top, resting them on a slab of brick placed on top of one of the burners of the big iron stove. She had two irons which she placed on the hot surface of the stove and traded off between them, as one would cool off, she switched to a hot one, always with a heavy cloth around the handle to keep from burning her hand, she ironed until it was time to switch again. Blake never realized she worked so hard. He just wore clean ironed clothes with no thought of how they got that way.

He wiled away the hours in his room going through his treasure box, which held balls of string, assorted by colors and width, marbles, old toy soldiers, special white feathers found in unusual places and when least expected, (which he thought to be angels trying to get his attention, by reminding him they were still watching over him), also several devil's pocketbooks (black sacs with four pointed corners, the birth sac for skates), a shark's tooth, several carvings from Mingin, his own collection of lost baby teeth and a few small crystals he found in the cave. It seemed that each of the children found them. They looked like the magic crystals Poseidon had given them, but these crystals seemed to have no special powers. However, they all kept them just in case, and now, his button from the Civil War.

On one of the days, he had carried down from the attic the book on knives and guns, drawn by Uncle Jabez or Aunt Rhetta. These fascinated him, and he was intent on memorizing the various types. He wanted to be a knife specialist. He also pulled from under his bed the beautiful jade dragon he had claimed from the chest they found under the waterfall. The one left with Uncle Jabez for safe-keeping by Captain Graham Johns. He intended to give it to his mother when the time was right. Maybe her birthday. He needed time to think of how to explain how and where he got it. He didn't think that his mom would appreciate the "pirate chest" story.

Also, knowing it was Blake, he used the opportunity to sneak into Luke's room and look around; he touched nothing, but curiosity was getting to him. He also did the same in Ellie's room, but that was so girly he hardly even took a look, nothing here but dolls, an old chain-mail pocket book, yellowish long gloves, a silver hand mirror, and other things of Aunt Rhetta's she found in the trunk, everything was so old. Ellie's room was boring. But, it took away the hours. Meanwhile, Theo seemed to think he was also on restriction, as he positioned himself on the roof near Blake's window every evening to sleep and to be ready for trouble should it come. He was getting used to his master and the many ways he could find to get himself in difficult situations.

Grandmom was so impressed with Blake helping her, that she thought he had earned his release from the dreaded house confinement.

About three days had passed when Grandmom approached Charlie as they sat in the living room together, her reading the Bible, and he listening to Edward R. Murrow, who began his program with "We cannot defend freedom abroad, by deserting it at home".

"Charlie, that little boy has been so good being confined to the house. I know it has only been three days, but the weekend is coming up, and I know the other two will miss him terribly if they have to play without him. Do you know he has helped me with the clothes, both washing and ironing, cleaned the chicken coop, collected eggs, tended to my flowers, and I can't tell you what else. Of course I enjoy him helping, but each afternoon, he slowly climbs those stairs and goes to his room, I just can't take the sadness anymore. Please allow him to finish his punishment before the weekend. I'm asking you to reconsider."

Pop looked at his sweet wife, sitting there with the Bible on her lap and tears in her eyes. Now, how could he refuse that?

"Odessa, you are a very persuasive woman. How can I say no? You tell him."

"No, Charlie, you tell him, he loves you so much, I can't imagine taking away the pleasure of seeing his face when you tell him. Don't be so harsh, I know you want him to be free to be with the others also." Odessa said, half-way stern.

So it was to be.

The kids came home from school on Friday afternoon and threw their books into their rooms, and Luke and Ellie ran out to groom the horses, Blake's also. When Grandpop got home, he went straight to Blake's room and found him spread out across the bed, looking at the ceiling with baseball glove in hand, tossing and catching a baseball in the air while singing *Deep in the Heart of Texas*. Each time he got to the chorus he punctuated it with a loud…BAM BAM BAM BAM.

"Well, Well, Well! Look who likes to sing. Now son, let me give you something to sing about, the others are out brushing their horses, and they are going to also take care of yours, I think you should go out and groom your own. What do you think?" Grandpop grinned a wide grin and flashed a wink.

Blake sat straight up in his bed and looked at his grandfather's eyes, while knitting his forehead into a questioning scowl as he searched his grandpop's face.

"Does that mean I can go outside?" he asked suspiciously.

"Sure does, you've done your time in solitary enough, and I miss your smiling face," and before his grandfather could finish, Blake was standing in the middle of the bed, and wrapped himself like a snake around his grandfather's neck.

Pulling his grip loose, Charlie laughed, and smacked him on the butt, "O.K., get goin' before they get to Spirit. Something tells me he is missing that face too."

He hardly saw the streak that was Blake as he jumped off the bed, hit the floor and out the door he went. He raced through the kitchen to the back door with that same speed, and on the run, not even hitting the steps, he yelled, "Thanks Grandmom! I know it was you!" The last three words were said on ground next to the back porch steps as he was now at full speed.

When Blake showed himself in the barn, the other two cheered, jumped up and down, and gave him a big hug. Then they handed him the brush and said, "Start working on your own horse!" And quick as that, restriction was over!

Easter break was upon them. After much plotting, scheming and giggling, the three sat in Blake's closet on the floor, where they did their best thinking, as they conspired to go back into the caves. This time, full on prepared, with Luke having taken a bucket to the beach to gather up tar used for dipping the torches he had placed around the dark walls. They would be comfortable knowing they had light.

After Blake's adventure, the off-shore U-boat crews, bored from waiting, sweating and stinking in their tight quarters, were once again sharing the binoculars to spy on the kids. Cautious to keep their distance this time, they only looked, and some daydreamed of going home. There was one more task they had to do on land, and to be honest, they were anxious about it. The lesson they learned last time they came ashore, and they did so more than the islanders knew, was that this was an unusual island. Not like anything they knew in Germany. They were beginning to be afraid of the kids. And what was a pack of wolves doing patrolling the shore? They were reminded of the horror tales they read about creatures in the *Grimm's Fairy Tales*. Could some of this be true, or just a story to scare kids from going into the woods? This island was a nightmare, and somehow the 100,000 tons of kill for the Knight's Cross seemed less than desirable.

After an especially active night, the birds still sang on the hill in Trent Woods, as spring was moving in. Mom's flowers in the ground, were waiting for the April rains to pop out their pretty heads. The garden was beginning to show itself also. What a strange oxymoron this was shaping up to be. Letters from Bill Finnegan were full of adventure, but not much on danger. He did not talk of war or peril, he gave no indication of where he was, letters could be intercepted from a downed ship or airplane, and classified information was not allowed. He was really trying to avoid worrying Nett and Grandmom, but they could see what he was up against, right out their window, and a nightly letter of encouragement was sent to him, also not detailing anything that was happening. The saying "loose lips sink ships" was never more true. It was forbidden to allow a sailor to pass along a secret to other sailors, thus causing total panic in places far removed from this island. Nett just talked about the kids and the horses, nothing about the spanking, lest he should ask why? It was all in all a stressful time for everyone.

Pop spent most of his spring vacation doing community business, Grandmom doing household chores, for which Blake held a new respect. He also knew that at night, or in the evening after her chores were finished, she sat down in Pop's study and wrote to all the boys, Blake saw her do that every day. Nett was just being social with all the young ladies of the villages, who did their best to occupy their attention away from their husbands, brothers, fathers, and their plight, and cautioned each other not to divulge anything going on in the ocean off the island. The kids were left pretty much to their own, and sort of were expected to be away from the house. It was an island after all, no shoes, no worries.

As springtime did its thing, spiders, cobwebs, snakes and other creatures hibernating over the winter began to emerge into the open, just
like the kids. Luke had a plan to keep Ellie safe and brave enough to go
into the dark cavern without the fear of creatures on the floor or in her
hair. His collection of tar in a bucket was one of the items designed to
be transported down the steps and behind the waterfall. This time there
was a lot of stuff to be moved into the cave in order to be ready for their
adventure. He did not worry about snakes; the wolves took care of that.
But his plan for creepy crawly things was genius, though what he didn't
know was that even though it was a good plan, he was going to need a
little bit of magic to pull it off. He was quite sure he had divine interven-
tion going for him.

Finally, they completed the task of transferring needed items to the
area behind the waterfall. They could tell they were under the "tree of life",
so named by them because of the seven huge branches. Here they could
see seven huge roots hugging the roof of the cave near the waterfall. Once
there, Luke explained his plan.

"O.K., I am going to make sure you don't worry about things crawling
on you," he said to Ellie. "Now, what you have to do is get all the wolves
to come sit right here with us, cause we don't want them to get hurt or to
scare them. There's gonna be a little bit of fire, and they have to trust us.
Can you make that clear also?" He knew it was a tall order, but if he was
ever going to know the extent of Ellie's powers, now was the time.

"Wha'cha gonna do?" Ellie was really confused.

"I'm gonna burn off all the spider-webs and get rid of any bats." He put
his hands on his hips and faced her. "Now, all you have to do is communicate with the wolves, all of them, even pups, even ones we don't know,
think them to come to you, I know you can do it, Blake and I will help."

"How'm I gonna do that?" she asked.

"You're gonna transmit a request to them, not loud, but your inside
call, the one in your mind, and Blake and I will think with you. What

words are you gonna use?" He needed to know exactly, so he and Blake could imagine the same thing.

"Les-see," she drawled out while she was considering how to use her inside mind. "What about saying, Twylah, come to me, bring all the other wolves in the caves including pups."

"Well that is kinda long, can't you think of anything else, shorter?" This time it was Blake, who really thought he couldn't remember all that, especially in the right order.

"Nope." She was adamant and closed her eyes.

Nothing for the other two to do but close their eyes and hold hands hoping they got it all straight.

Only a couple of minutes went by and they heard the clicking of nails and soft pad of paws, coming down the rocky floor of the cave. Opening their eyes, they were shocked at the sight. They could even smell them there were so many, and sitting at attention before their eyes were Twylah, Rafe, and Theo, also about six little furry balls at their feet, and under their bellies, as the pups snuggled close to their elders, and tried to sit at attention. One fell over, and as he had done once before, Luke reached down to shield him from the stream trickling down through the slanted floor from the waterfall. Blake moved Luke aside, and took his place as protector of the pups and stood silently awaiting this miracle Luke had devised. He too wanted all the crawly things gone. As they were positioning the pups, more adult wolves came to sit near them, bringing along a string of pups. The kids were afraid to play with them, not knowing what human scent would do on their fur, but the pups were drawn to the youngsters, maybe recognizing them, and crawled all over their feet. The kids had a giggle fit and almost forgot what they were there to do. This huge mansion area at the top of the tall hill was literally bursting with wolves. All were different colors and combinations of fur, but none as striking as the colors of the three that had adopted the chosen children.

Luke lit one of the torches, and as the others watched, and the wolves paid attention, he lightly touched the torch to one of the webs above him. Miraculously it lit up, and like some kind of silver thread, began to follow itself through the ceiling, and down through the cave. It was magical, like a sparkly string moving quietly across the ceiling, dropping small crystal balls to the floor, the smaller ones fizzled and went out. It was beautiful.

In the distance, they could hear the flapping of dark wings, and screeching of the smelly bats as they hurried out of the way of the string of fire. The bats flew away from the kids, giving them the realization that there must be an exit or opening to this long dark cave. Finally, silence. Luke then lit a couple of the torches he had left on the wall, and walked a little farther away, lit some more, and turned around for all to follow. The wolves just got up and walked down the cave to wherever they came from; the kids could hear the playful barks of the pups as they followed, rolling around tussling with each other as they went. Then they too were gone.

Luke shone the light up so that they could see it was a clear path of dirt and clay above them, no webs, no spiders. The fire sparkled on the walls of the limestone and shell packing put there by former inhabitants. It was like the Milky Way lighting the ceiling and bouncing off the walls, then slowly losing its luster, only to be picked up once again as the kids began to move around and explore. It seemed warmer after the fire string, and they discovered there were so many openings on either side where maybe families stayed during a storm or invasion over the hundreds of years the Croatoan occupied that area. His idea had worked, but not without the help of his saint Micah, whose idea it was to begin with. Micah was also interested in watching the kids explore the deep dark caverns of Underground Buxton, so he had put the idea into Luke's mind and waited.

As they went into the first alcove off the main path of the cave, they discovered that there were stone benches along the walls, maybe for sleeping. The ante-rooms were dank and smelled of earth, 'not very pleasant for sleeping,' they thought. In others, they found chards of pots they knew were like the ones used at the cooking fires of Weroansquoa, and Powwaw. Blake swore one of the rooms must have belonged to Mingin as he kicked up a very sharp stone that would cut anything. There were sketches on the walls, they did not stop to examine them thoroughly. Maybe they told a story, and maybe it was a sign of someone with a special talent for drawing. However, they recognized the turtle, wolves, and ravens, and a mighty eagle, only one. Maybe that was not something the Indians saw in the sky, possibly in a trance, the kids had never seen an eagle on the island. Celebratory masks were drawn, but their meaning was obscure. Some looked menacing, and others looked like deities. On one wall, for the length of the room was what they recognized as Dawnland, with the sun either rising or setting, it was unclear which. On one wall was a whale, and on another several sharks, and men with spears poised to strike. They were mostly done in a chalky substance, or some lighter stone, and were now very dull, though the kids could make out the subject of the sketch. With the wolves leading the way they reached a widening of the cave, more dug out, and rounded with sort of rocks along the edge, they imagined it to be an area for conference, or communal meetings. Here they had gone as far as they dared and decided to start back, each with their torches searching the ground, walls and if possible, the roof.

As they traveled the path, several things became apparent, the Croatoan were big believers in crystals, and had embedded several along all the paths, thus lighting the way, also, being followers of water, the children noticed the water trickle had become a stream, and they could tell they were on a downward slant. It was also getting much colder the farther they went, and they knew any further and they would need heavier clothing.

They discussed on the way back, as they extinguished each torch, the outerwear they would bring and store in one of the farthest caves to put on when it started to get chilly. All the while, they could hear water overhead. They were either traveling under the ocean, or the sound, their inner direction was now confused. All of what they saw they discussed, remembering what kind of life the Croatoans had led. There was much to see, but this was the first day. There were six more days of vacation, not counting Palm Sunday or Easter Sunday. Boy, was this going to be an adventure! They were determined to find the end and knew they must stay together and not wander off.

When they finally got back to the waterfall, Rafe and Theo were lounging around in the water, and only slightly moved over as the kids broke their way through. Twylah was following behind. They were now wet, and cold, and hurried up the steps to the inside walls of the house and the fireplace in Uncle Jabez's bedroom, with plans to start a fire, as soon as they were on the other side. When they got warm they would then sneak down the stairs to their rooms. They made it, it was not yet dark, and they could smell something in the kitchen that made them even hungrier. Ellie decided she would go sit with Grandmom, to give the boys some time. Grandmom felt her wet hair, shook her head and smiled. Her *knowing* was kicking in, and Ellie smiled back. Some things did not need to be discussed.

"Did you talk to Weroansquoa today?" Grandmom asked.

Ellie couldn't answer at first, then said, also with a *knowing* smile, "it felt like it."

At the supper table Grandpop had a surprise. "How would you young-uns like to go up to Rodanthe on Thursday with me? There is something I need to talk with Cap'n Levine about, and since you know him, and Fonzie, I thought you'd like to tag along. It would be good for you to play with ol' Fonzie, he's getting on in years, and might enjoy the company. Levene told me to bring you, he knows how you like to ride with me, and since we don't have a dog, it could be fun. Ol' Fonz knows his way around and will probably show you the station while I talk to the Captain."

There was a resounding "YES!" all the way around. Both boys wanted to see the pictures of the surfmen on the wall and hear what was happening off the coast in Rodanthe. They wondered if anyone else was going through the war like they were.

Grandmom was at her best for supper, someone had given Pop a mess of big fish, and she had made a huge pan with potatoes and somewhere she had gotten some apples. Quite a delicacy in these times but leave it to Capt'n Charlie. He was always bringing home the best.

"What did you explorers do today?" he asked.

"Explored," Luke answered as he took another plateful of potatoes and fish. He could tell they were having apple cake, he saw a smear of it on Grandmom's apron.

It was a beautiful Palm Sunday, and after church, the family relaxed on the porch. This day, the kids decided to take ol' Tony and Big Roy to the beach. These animals also needed to wallow in the surf to rid themselves of whatever insects had been biting them. It was a joy to see the huge Morgan horses wade in the surf, they actually played. Blake and Ellie got on Big Roy, and Luke on ol' Tony, and they also took them south down the beach, they were hoping the tar would be less there, but it seemed there was as much there as on the north end. When tankers were torpedoed, their oil just collected together in the cool ocean, and washed to shore in lumps. Would their beach ever be clear and white again? Even when they stopped to pick up a shell, it showed signs of being dirtied with thick oil, and mixed with sand, these shells were not fit to take home to Grandmom.

The kids tried not to be sad, but they wished the war would end. Two more ships were struck that night. It seemed the Germans never took a vacation or celebrated the religious holidays with everyone else. Was there no end to their desire to kill? This night several men were saved as a lifeboat made it to shore without holes, and the occupants, this time, from Brazil, were helped to shore in this foreign land, without the benefit of translator, kindness spoke a language not necessary to translate. It seemed to overcome both their uneasiness and their plight. The second ship went down with no survivors.

The next day was overcast, it was unclear if the smoke was manmade or if the weather had changed, as everyone could smell the destruction coming from the sea. Pop could hear the engines from the *USS Roper*, going back and forth, looking for U-boats or survivors, or floating sailors clinging to damaged wood. Evidently there were none.

Luke and Blake spent their time getting ready for a return to the caves the following day. Now he knew what he needed. He gathered rope, and took enough to wrap around both his and Blake's one shoulder. They gathered flashlights and checked the batteries. They took out the old ones, even though not spent, and put in new ones. Blake got his knife, of course he had his flints, and they found one of Pop's long knives used for chopping weeds, it was called a machete. Luke made a leather bag for it from an old rawhide boot he found and had been saving. He cut off the shoe of it and fastened the end so that it was closed. He cut some wide cloth and made a sling that would fit on Ellie's back, she could sling it over both shoulders and have it hanging down her back, so it would neither be heavy, nor in the way. She was just the carrier; the machete would be used by one of the boys for chopping down roots or bushes in their way. They knew they were going into an area they had not yet explored.

Since Ellie had spoken to Weroansquoa and gotten her powers, she had visibly grown stronger. Her blood did not freely run from scratches as before, and her attitude had changed. Actually, they all had grown more aware with age. Each gathered their whips, (Ellie had spent time over the last year practicing in the woods with hers. She had taken Twylah with her, and while the boys were off on their own, she was wanting to surprise them). She did on this day, as she pulled out hers, and strapped it to her belt along with the boys.

"Where'd you get that?' Blake was shocked.

Luke turned to see what he was talking about and saw the big smile of satisfaction on her face, as she patted the woven strings of hide at her side, and just said "Never mind."

Now they all three had one, but it was questionable whether or not Ellie could use hers.

Blake took out his favorite knife and started practicing throwing it against the pilings in the barn. He drew back to make his third throw, and all of a sudden, Ellie took her whip, and easily and correctly snapped it out of his hand.

"Wow!" Luke said. "Somebody's been practicing."

Then it was an all-out contest, hardly anything hanging in the barn was exempt from somebody wrapping a whip around it. Getting ready was as fun as going. Maybe more, they didn't know yet. But all this, along with the wolves who would not leave their side in the cave, there was probably nothing they should be afraid of.

Luke took out his bow and arrows, and put the quiver on his back, and hooked the bow to the rope on his shoulder. Added to all this, they took coats, gloves, and a jar of Grandmom's fig preserves. Blake filled old Pepsi bottles with water and capped them off with corks carved from broken bobbing corks used for indicating the position of fish nets on the sound. These he put in a bag and fashioned the bag over his other shoulder. They were ready!

They went far underground, on a search for the end of the cave. Where did those bats go? They had plans to go as far as they could, without stopping to see if they could find the end. After what seemed like forever, they were far underground traveling under the Buxton Woods, although they did not know it. It was so large it could have been a separate village, but why would anyone live here when they had such a beautiful island above to grow their crops and catch the bounty from the sea?

As they traveled on ground they had not yet trod, the floor of the cave became littered with broken limbs and rotten leaves and twigs. The cave widened considerably, and the walls looked to be made of hard earth, rather than limestone and shells as the entrance of the cave had been, the roots of the trees protruded from the top and sides, hindering their passageway. Some roots they hacked away, others seemed to join themselves together as one living tree gave life to a faltering tree above ground.

This part of the cave appeared more natural than the man-made entrance from the house, and it was not long before they encountered a stream of water, fed from the underground. It led into a small pool fed from the many artesian springs on the island. It was the same water that the villagers sank wells to access, and the same that supplied the Croatoans. The sound of water grew more prominent, and the smell of water was strong, as they cautiously went forward. Seeing the wolves drink from the pool made them aware that they were safely near water without salt.

Luke carried both a flashlight and his bucket of tar, keeping a sharp eye out for the flickering of the torches. It was his responsibility to see that they did not run out of light.

Ellie stepped in a puddle of water and looked down to find a deeper stream than they had encountered before. The light on the stream was beautiful, and as she was getting ready to tell the others "Hey! Watch out!" Blake yelled, right in front of her was a pool, and, on further inspection it was deep. Then they found it, a small stream of water, not a waterfall, but a rush of water coming from the roof. Buxton was known for fresh water aquifers, and the Croatoan also built access to fresh water when they found it. In many places fresh water seeped out of the sand, on its way to a larger stream. When the kids got closer around the pool, careful with their steps, they could see shards of light coming from the roof of the cave. Water dripped from above, nourishing the extended tree roots and making them pliable. Then the light got more prominent and they could see glimmers of the sky. They smelled the water, but they could also smell something else. The beach. There was definitely the distinct smell of the salty ocean. Fresh water was coming from the opening in the roof of the cave, this water also had its own distinct smell, for some reason, it smelled fresh. The water that fed the roots also collected into the pool.

Seeing the slivers of light from above, Ellie closed her eyes, the streaks of blue and silver light streamed in from everywhere. They could see that this was a part of the cave that did not display carvings, it was not ceremonial, it was something else. The light danced on the water of the pool, the torches lit the sides of the cave, and the boys saw that Ellie had closed her eyes. They sat down beside her, and also closed their eyes; whatever Ellie was seeing, they wanted to see also. They reached out their hands to connect with her and add strength to whatever was becoming a reality in her mind. The blue and silver light also revealed something else as it danced up the walls. Following the beam from the torches, they saw that the cave had widened more than they thought, and the roof seemed to be higher. Maybe there had once been more water that flowed through. Something shone on the walls, and the children realized that there were crystals embedded in the walls. They extinguished the torches in favor of the light given off by the crystals.

Ellie rose, unloosening her grip on the boys, and retrieved three of the crystals, one for each of them. She handed one to Blake and one to Luke, the third she tucked into the fold of her sleeve so that the crystal touched her skin. Then she again took a free hand of each boy. The white wolf approached and nestled down next to Ellie and she leaned against the comfortable furry body. Once again Ellie closed her eyes and the boys followed, looking on were the three saints, Travis, Micah and Brendan. There were nine, the children, their saints and their wolves. As they traveled away from the entrance, the other wolves wandered away, leaving only Rafe, Theo and Twylah.

The children experienced a vision not unlike the visions displayed from the magic book that Uncle Jabez had written about the Pirates. Could Aunt Rhetta have put a spell on this part of the cave? She must have known about it, she was always with her wolf, learning the nature of the woods and waters of the island. These crystals were also similar to the ones Poseidon had given the kids allowing them to breathe underwater, just not as large.

They were not round, but irregularly shaped. As water dripped down from the roots above, they wondered if it was raining. The wetter the roots got, the more pliable they were, no longer stiff and dry, their connections to each other began to spread in patterns. It was through these patterns and the openings between them that several small caverns were revealed in the walls of the cave. Ellie noticed a twinkle between the roots, coming from the holes they formed. She stepped closer to observe what shone from the small indentations. To her surprise the largest cavity contained a most familiar object, Weroansquoa's pearl, the one she wore as a crown.

The boys also stepped forward to examine the spaces between the root openings, and discovered more pearls, some small and bunched together, some in strange shapes. These were the treasures from the shell middens the Indians combed for ceremonies. What they did not use, they stored in these crevices. They gave light to the cave and against the torch, sparkled off the pool of water, taking on the colors of blue, green and lavender. These pearls had been polished.

Luke's wolf, Rafe, nudged him, the first time he had ever voluntarily touched his human, and as Luke turned, he saw the figure of Powwaw, ghost-like, almost see-through, the top half was clearly seen, but the bottom of the figure was obscure, vague. He was wearing his ceremonial robe and holding his walking stick. Theo moved closer to Blake, and as he touched the large animal's fur, he too saw the ghost-like figure of Mingin, holding out a beautifully carved piece of dark coral in the shape of a Raven. As Ellie touched the large pearl, she was visited by the apparition of her beloved Weroansquoa. The three shamans floated near their chosen child, and somehow everyone was able to communicate. Now the twelve of them, spirits, children, wolves and apparitions watched as the active tree roots spread apart even more revealing an opening to what was hidden at the end of the cave.

As they walked forward on the crushed leaves through the opening the roots had concealed, the crystals picked up the blue and silver light that completely surrounded them.

The saints hovered at the top of the new cavern, also leading the way. Each child kept a hand on their wolf for comfort and protection, from what, they did not understand. They knew only to trust their animal guardians and their ghostly shaman. They also knew that wolves would growl if there was anything to avoid. The animals made the children brave and allowed them to follow their curiosities.

World War I

The children continued trusting their wolves for protection, and accepting the lead of their ghostly friends, as they moved closer and closer to the sound of crashing waves, and the smell of the fresh ocean breeze, which now was unencumbered by the smell of smoke and death. They stood under the clay roof of the cave held together by tightly entwining tree roots. The large opening revealed a small white sandy beach. That was the water they heard. As the company, real and unreal, stepped to the edge of the opening they observed another apparition floating away, over the ocean. The new figure had on flowing dark robes, he had long white hair and a thick beard. He was a familiar sight. It was Suki, the rejected shaman of the Croatoan tribe. He held a staff which resembled a snake. It was what he carried the last time they saw him. This was evil, moving over the ocean to connect with other evils that now existed in their world.

The children, still touching their very own crystals, and Ellie with Weroansquoa's pearl in her pocket, their hands still touching their wolf, stepped out onto the small beach. They turned to speak with their spiritual apparitions, hoping for them to explain the presence of Suki, and they saw the wisps fade backwards behind the roots as they once more thickened. Before he completely disappeared, Powwaw tossed something to Luke. It was a black pearl. Luke stared into his hand at the magnificent treasure and wondered if it meant something. The black pearl, though not as valuable as the large pearl of Weroansquoa, protects the owner from negative energy, carries healing powers, is the symbol for hope and is also considered a symbol of wisdom. Like Ellie, he put it in his pocket, he needed more time to think and to research.

The beach was welcoming, and for a second, the three stood and watched as it produced wave after wave of foamy lacy white salt froth, each wave slowly returning to form another. It was the first time in a long time they had seen clear water, not marred by war. They were awakened to the present, still holding their crystals. Ellie felt in her pocket, the pearl was still there. Luke was not ready to show his treasure, it was too personal to him.

Looking around, they could tell that they were in Buxton, on the beach which adjoined the beginning of the Buxton woods. They were north of the path they had made from the beach to the mansion. They were located on the peak of the hill under which they had just explored. The maritime forest that made up the Buxton and Trent woods was thick and lay at the north end of the tall hill where the mansion was built. On the inside road, there was a clear break of the thick trees that indicated the end of one village and the beginning of the other, but here, on the beach, everything was connected.

Stunned by what they had just experienced, the three sat down on the first rise of dune they came to. They needed a minute to reflect on the several truly astonishing experiences that had just been witnessed in the cave. In their hands, they had the evidence, in their minds, they felt the presence of their personal shamans, they knew they were protected. Their wolves sat at the foot of the dune behind them, out of sight, but ready to respond if needed.

Did they really see Suki? Was he a part of the evil in the ocean? Had he not disappeared while standing at the edge of the waters where two great currents collided? What did it all mean? They felt a little conflicted, should they be afraid of Suki? But, had they not seen him driven from the cave? They held hands again, and closed their eyes to regain a connection, this time for calm. They did not want their cave experience to have been scary. Then, after a few minutes, Ellie squeezed the boy's hands. Opening their eyes, the blue and silver clouds were clearly seen in the sky, and they formed the shape of a raven. Blake felt in his pocket and found the carved raven Mingin had given him. He smiled, showed it to the others, and vowed to never again be without it. Ellie had the pearl, Blake the raven, and Luke found himself in possession of two stones, one the pearl, and another, a surprise, which had several colors, resembling an opal. He did not remember anyone giving it to him, but he did remember the beautiful colors of the pool, and actually, he did scoop up some of the water with his hand. Did that form a solid stone? This was once again a physical reminder of their connection to the spiritual world.

Once home, they were exhausted, and all went upstairs for a nap. Grandmom *knew* but explained to Nett that napping was a good thing during vacation, and their mother should possibly just let them sleep. By suppertime, all were up, rested and very hungry. Tonight they were having baked chicken, sweet potatoes from the garden and lemon meringue pie.

The following day, thoughts of the cave now satisfied, they knew they did not want to take another vacation day underground. That night was punctuated by more window rattling from the heavy firing of torpedoes at sea keeping them awake. So, the children were late getting up. Even their grandfather took the vacation time to sleep late, the thought of possibly providing assistance in the rescue effort had caused him to once again go with the other men to the station and help out most of the night.

At breakfast, the conversation went back to war, how could they help it, it was so paramount in everyone's mind.

"Grandpop you keep saying World War II. Why do you call it two? Do we go to war all the time, and are they are numbered?' Blake was just getting the nerve to ask. He always accepted the name, but all of a sudden, the number was curious to him.

"Son, no, we do not go to war all the time, this one is called two, because it was the second time we had to go to war against the same country. Remember when we were talking about all the countries making alliances with each other, and when one country is challenged, it seems like the others, in order to honor their loyalty, line up against the one who disrespects their partner? Haven't you ever taken up for a friend who was being bullied? Well, just make it bigger. Two countries are allies, and an opponent starts a fight with a country you have sworn to protect. That's when nations honor their agreement to stand behind their pact by stepping up to protect the one they support. That's what happened when we went to war the first time against Germany." Pop knew he was in for another long talk.

"O.K.," he added, "didn't we agree that we would not discuss war at the table?"

Blake got a long face and dropped his head. It seemed that he just could not keep out of trouble with his beloved Pop. He had just made up with him after the deal with the German U-boat sailors, and now here he was again, starting to irritate his tired grandfather. He knew he needed to shut-up. He also could tell when Luke hit him under the table with his foot. Blake tried to act like that didn't hurt, but it was certainly a hard enough rap to get his attention.

"Sorry Pop, I forgot, and I don't want to talk about it anyway. I know how tired you are with all you are having to do, so please just forget I said anything. Pop, do you think it would be safe for me to take Spirit on the beach today? It's getting hot, and the flies and mosquitoes are beginning to bother him. Used to, when we lived at the lighthouse, I could take my horse on the beach to roll around in the surf and get rid of the itchy fly bites. Are we ever going to get to do that again?" Blake was changing the subject as fast as his little brain could latch on to something. He had already decided to take Spirit on the beach, he was just going to do it. Before, he had no intentions of asking anyone. Before, no one cared. He was used to spending every day with his horse, they all did. But, out of courtesy, this time he asked.

"Yeh, Pop, Gus is biting at himself, I guess he eats the flies, they need to roll around in the salt water. We all miss those times on the beach. It seems like all the bad stuff happens at night, and maybe after Easter we can just go right after school, if we are together, we probably won't get in trouble." Luke thought that would be a good idea and was surprised that Blake came up with it.

"Me too Pop, Blue misses the ocean. We don't think those people are going to come near *our* house again. Can we? Pleeease?" Ellie was now interested in what was being discussed as she looked up from one of her favorite breakfast and fried cornbread, fried eggs and grits. Pop was eating his favorite, a couple of one minute eggs still in the shell which he ate from a small egg shaped cup. The kids liked to see him lop off the top and eat the egg from the shell.

Cap'n Charlie looked at Odessa, then Nett, trying to figure if it was a good idea or a trick. It seemed lately he couldn't tell the difference.

"Remember we are going to get up early tomorrow, Chicamacomico is a long way away, and we need to catch low tide. They all shook their heads and sneaked big smiles as they made eye contact with each other. They truly were not planning anything questionable, unlike most other times. They were just missing the horses and felt guilty for having spent so much time with the wolves in the cave, keeping them from doing anything with the horses. After all, the wolves always got to go, even when the horses went. From past experience it was everybody's feeling that the wolves were needed for protection. Luke had at one time thought to follow the path of the cave above ground through the Buxton Woods, but his grandfather had always warned him that those woods were full of poisonous cotton-mouthed moccasins, and as it was a favorite place for hunting, the men wore heavy high boots, in case they encountered one. So, he was not about to venture into that area, and he did not yet have heavy hunting boots. He thought to get them, the same time he got his first rifle, but he was a year or so away from that. He was never afraid of varmints in the cave, the wolves took care of that.

The next morning, early, before daybreak, the darkened car left the hill heading south to the Creeds Hill station south of Trent, where they could cross over to the beach and the hard sand of low tide. It was so dark, the children wondered how Pop could see, as lights on the island were out, and there was only a sliver of a moon for guidance, a full moon would have exposed them. Pop thought the U-boats would not bother with them, even if they saw a single car they would not waste shots from guns on the deck of the sub, knowing it would give away their position, and, they were after bigger targets. But, if they had known who was riding in that car, should they have seen it, he felt sure they would have destroyed the little boy and his family who had been responsible for the sinking of one of their own.

The trip was long, and they passed several men on horseback, as the coast guard had brought horses to the island from Texas, also experts to teach the coast guard and sailors how to ride. The horses and men were for use in patrolling the shore along the beach knowing that horses see better at night. The military was anxious about men coming ashore, also the possibility of men who needed to be rescued from a stricken ship. The horses were kept in pens near Kinnakeet. The Texans got busy teaching other guardsmen how to ride. The men volunteered for the duty and learned fast during their afternoon riding lessons. Now the beach was full of them. Usually riding in pairs, they were armed, and ready to shoot anyone they did not know, so Cap'n Charlie had alerted everyone where he was going, when he was leaving, who he carried with him, and who he was destined to see. They pulled over from the beach at Kinnakeet to pick up Charlie Williams, a friend of both Charlie Gray, and Levene Midgett. It appeared this was an important meeting of communities. Also meeting them there was Maurice Burrus, and a couple of others plus the Chief of the Coast Guard station from Hatteras. The cars did not leave at the same time, nor follow each other as would have happened on former days. Dawn was a time the U-boats were just finishing their hunt, and the men of the villages were on a mission. They gambled on a certain amount of danger but thought their venture was needed.

The children tried not to sleep, even as the fresh breeze from the morning and the car gently rocking as it rumbled over the camel backs of the sand near the shore made them drowsy. They forced themselves to stay awake to see the new and interesting debris on the beach. They passed horses with sailors on patrol, this was not a time fall asleep and miss anything. They did not utter a word. If they had something to say, it was with hand signals, thinking ahead, Ellie had sense enough to bring pencil and paper. They were allowed to use the bathroom at Mr. Charlie William's house, who crawled into the car with goodies for the children courtesy of Miss Ianthia, his wife. The treats were so good the children couldn't help but take a little nap and slept soundly until they pulled up over the beach to Rodanthe. Taking a nap was a mistake, it made them wide awake and ready to talk, but with kicks and punches, Ellie reminded them to keep quiet, this was a trip they were only "allowed" to go on.

The men had their meeting for the entire morning, while the kids played with Cap'n Levene's huge Chesapeake Bay retriever, Fonzie, and also being entertained by Miss Cretia, the captain's wife. Finally, the men from Hatteras started back. They were first because they had longer to go, and they did not want to arouse suspicion. The war was right beside them lurking in the ocean waters off the beach. Everyone took that seriously.

Captain Levene had already met the children when he took them on a ride in the DUKW. He had invited Cap'n Charlie to bring them for

Fonzie, who never got to play with children, and old dogs needed that. Cap'n Levene singled out Blake, who looked like he had a question.

"What have you got to say for yourself young man, you seem to be brimming with questions, and I see you've grown up quite a bit." The captain smiled his generous smile.

"Uh-oo," Grandpop thought, "that was a mistake."

"Well, Pop and I were talking," Blake began and sounded so old! "I was wondering why we number our wars."

Captain Levene Midgett almost rolled out of his chair. As a respected elder of his village, he was always wanting to foster the education of young people, and Charlie Gray was known for his unusually quick grandchildren. He had also heard the girl was a little bit of a wonder. Right away he noticed the color of the children's eyes, Ellie's eyes were sea green, Blake's blue, and Luke had brown eyes. He couldn't help but think about Ellie's eyes, so very prominent, and striking in color. Did that contribute to her being as unusual as everyone said? He was happy to see them again. Word got around on the island, if something happened in Hatteras in the morning, Chicamacomico was well aware of it by noon. The captain was also good friends with Willis Burrus, as he had purchased a couple of horses from him, so he was in the mood for a yarn to tell about these remarkable children also.

The kids' first visit to ride on the DUKW was so full of excitement for everyone he had failed to concentrate on Cap'n Charlie's amazing children, but after hearing about their visits to choose horses from Willis, he made up his mind he would get to know them. He missed his own son who had recently died from a motorcycle accident while on leave from the service. After that, he did not hesitate to listen to the laughter of children.

"Well, of course it really wasn't our first war, there was one we call WWI, but we usually were fighting nearer to home, and always had our hands full of trouble here. But this was our first time fighting across the sea. Tell you the truth son, it kinda started down your way."

At that, Cap'n Charlie, volunteered to take Williams out to see the DUKW, and, if there were any sailors to be found, he was hoping he might get to crawl up in it again. He had bragged about it so much.

Blake sat on the floor beside Cap'n Levene , he leaned against the wall of the station, with his arm over Fonzie, who seemed perfectly content to stretch out comfortably. Luke and Ellie were in rocking chairs on the porch, as was Captain Levene Midgett, friend of both their grandfather and also President Franklin Roosevelt, who had had so much respect for the Midgett's and the area, he directed Captain Levene to put the DUKW through its paces on this unforgiving sandy island. Coming to this island was a test of the vehicle's readiness for use on the Pacific islands now being attacked by the Japanese. Roosevelt wanted to determine if this vehicle was capable for use in extracting our men from an island if need be.

"I know you kids lived near the lighthouse for years, and you know why we have the lighthouse. But have you ever heard about the Lightship that is anchored near the Diamonds, which also warns ships to stay clear of danger?"

"I have," said Luke as he raised his hand as if in school, "My friend's grandfather, Mr. Walter Barnett, was on that ship."

"Yes, you young-uns at Buxton have a lot to do with the sea, so do our kids up here at Chicamacomico. We are mostly all about the sea, this is a village of men who take to the sea, and most make their living either on the sound or sea fishing and hunting. My family, the Midgett's, are surfmen. Many have been given medals for bravery saving others from the perils of the sea. My uncle Banister Midgett, was the first of my family to be distinguish as a surfman by the government. His has the first medal for bravery. Eventually metals were given to several of my cousins before me."

"But this story is about your friend's grandfather, Mr. Walter, who was the man in charge of the Lightship at that time. It was around 1918, exactly one year and some, after the United States declared war for the first time against Germany, the one we now call World War I," and he sneaked a wink at Blake. "We had tried to stay out of war, it wern't our war, or so we thought, but Germany was so bent on destroying the world she started to sink everything in the Atlantic, no matter what country it represented—it didn't make any difference if they were at war or not. Guess she was just assuming she was going to rule Europe, and the rest of the world should just be put on notice. Well, the United States, didn't take too kindly on the Germans with their new-fangled underwater killers to be targeting ships who were peaceful. Like us. And like countries south of here. We kind of let it go when she sank the passenger liner *Lusitania*, a British liner that left New York, going to England. It was carrying around two thousand passengers, mostly Europeans, and over a hundred Americans. Got her right off the coast of Ireland."

"Germany was sinking everything she could with those U-boats in the English Channel, also around the northern Atlantic. It was known that they were near Ireland, and England had warned the *Lusitania*, which was both carrying people plus several tons of ammunition and shells for the war effort. So, the combination of war supplies with passengers was a risk. The passengers leaving from New York were warned in the newspapers not to take that voyage, but the warning was ignored. We were not in the war that had been going on for about a year or so in Europe, so the American passengers paid no attention to the warning. Of course, they had not been informed that the ship, in addition to passengers was carrying ammunition for Great Britain."

"The captain of the ship was advised that the German U-boats were active near the coast of Ireland, and warned to change his course, to zig-zag, or take other tactical measures to confuse anyone tracking her so as not to be a casualty. He disregarded the warning, thinking his ship was faster than a sub, not considering the speed of a torpedo, which was impossible to outrun. When the torpedo hit, everything exploded, and with all that firepower on board, the ship went down in around fifteen minutes, taking everyone with it.

Blake was glued to the story.

"Boats from Ireland saved a little more'n 500, along with a few Americans, but it was a disaster, a terrible waste of life. They were innocents, not combatants. That was just about the last straw for us, but we still hesitated to declare war. We really tried to stay out of it."

"Germans kept torpedoing everything in the Atlantic, and finally we had no choice but to declare war. We never expected it to reach here, we were just going to help Great Britain out, and keep the fighting over there. But, then the loss of some of our citizens, and continued disrespect over the next three years, and our ships becoming targets, changed our minds. It was comin' to us whether we liked it or not. Everybody wants to knock off the leader, and we were surely a country to deal with. They musta thought to get us before we could be prepared."

"Cap'n, didn't those people put themselves in danger when they ignored the newspaper about not going? And wasn't the Captain also responsible? I don't mean to take up for those killers in Germany, but it seems like they warned us." Luke looked straight at Captain Levene, who thought, '*they say the girl is the smart one, they might have missed this kid*'. Then he smiled.

"Son, you are absolutely correct. But I have to tell you, with that Captain thinking his ship could outrun the Germans, sometimes cocky is mistaken for confidence, and he made a grave mistake. Guess it don't pay to put yourself ahead of better judgement. I will say this for him, he was one of the last ones off the ship."

"After that, and a few other strikes at American shipping, two years later in 1917, we felt we needed to jump in and help end this thing. That's when they came after us, here, in our own back yard. They knew then what they know now, that supplies have to pass the Diamonds to get on that river flowing straight to Europe. We call it the Gulf Stream, the Pirates during the time of their raids called it "the Spanish Main," it is a river in the middle of the ocean, and it is larger than the six largest rivers of the world combined."

"Amazon and Mississippi?" Blake really thought he had the fine Captain there.

"And then some! They say one thousand Mississippi's." he said.

A chorus of "Wow!" came from all three. They didn't realize they lived next to such a famous body of water.

"Well, if all these ships are moving in the same direction, on the same river, it was an obvious place to be, so they sent five of their U-boats to our shores, a few a little north of here, and two, right off our coast. Studying the map, they knew the ships had to pass Diamond Shoals to get into the Gulf Stream, and, if going straight to New York, the Wimble Shoals, right off the Rodanthe coast. The Gulf Stream also naturally flows by itself at about four miles an hour, making it easy on the ships riding it.

"When U-#140 got to Hatteras, they first fired on a merchant ship the *Merak*, who tried to out maneuver the torpedo and ran aground on the shoals. The men immediately abandoned ship, and that was when Walter saw them—it was hit pretty close to where the lightship sat. Cap'n Walter got on the telegraph and started warning incoming ships. "German sub in area, sinking ships."

The sub picked up the transmission as well and sent one back to Walter, "keep your fingers off that button or we'll shoot them off."

"I think Walter believed them but had more sand in him than anyone knew. He, at that point, put his own life on the line and continued to warn incoming ships. They say he saved more than twenty ships before they fired on his tower, then they sent another transmission ordering the men on the lightship to abandon ship or go down with it. Walter ordered his men off the lightship, just in time for the Germans to start firing. As they were trying to sink it, Walter and his men started rowing ashore.

"On the lightship were twelve men, six rowers and Walter at the stern with a 16ft sweep oar, one of the men was Guy Quidley, a fine man with an oar, both of 'em from Buxton, and five others with a bunch of 14ft oars and 'bout ten miles to row before reaching the shore near Cape Point. Guy broke two of those fourteen footers, and all the while the U-boat #140, kept firing at that lightship. Once in a while it aimed at Walter, but they were steady getting out of the way.

"Then U #140, came close to shore and shot out the lines of a couple of telephone poles which carried wire out from the Coast Guard station, preventing further communication. They say people in the village went down to the shore, after hearing the blasts, it was the first time they had ever heard such a ruckus coming from the ocean. The men from the Diamond Shoals lightship left around two o'clock in the afternoon and rowed to well after dark. I heard that Walter couldn't close his hands for a week after handling that oar and had to be fed by his wife all the while."

> *"We succeeded in getting away and never did mortal*
> *men row as we did that afternoon."*
> WALTER BARNETT

"I believe that, Cap'n Levene. I saw my Aunt Josephine feed Uncle Backey one time and wondered why such a grown man would let his wife feed him. Then Pop told me his hands were messed up, torn open blisters and swollen by having to row such a long time in the ocean on one of his off-shore rescues, he was also a surfman." This time it was Ellie.

"Yessir, little miss, your Uncle Baxter is one of the greatest; got himself a couple of gold medals for saving lives. I think he saved as many as 300 lives in his time on the water. He is a great man, you should be proud." Captain Levene knew Baxter Miller, and quite admired him as a man and as a surfman.

"So. that's how it started for us. That was lightship # 71, and # 72 was in action six months later, with Walter Barnett, the hero of #71 serving as first mate on that one. "U-boat # 140 sank three ships plus the lightship.

The crew of the *Merak* ran aground trying to get away, but U-boat #140 went back after they destroyed the lightship and filled her full of holes to make sure she sank. Those men abandoned their ship before the sub got back to them. The U-boat wanted to make sure the *Merak* didn't gain the water again. Nine days after the lightship, U-boat #117 fired on a British tanker, the *Mirlo*, right off here. Serving in the Coast Guard at the Chicamacomico lifesaving station was a cousin of mine, John Allen Midgett Jr. whose father had served in the same capacity before him."

About that time, Charlie Gray and Charlie Williams came wandering back to the station to help their friend Levene Midgett cope with the children and found him in the middle of the story about saving the British ship *Mirlo*. Neither man wanted to interrupt their friend as he told the story of a lifetime, about one of the "mighty Midgett's," John Allen Midgett Jr. They both knew the story but wanted to hear Levene tell it. Both Ellie and Luke immediately arose and gave their rockers to the men and took a seat on the bench nearby. Blake looked up from stroking a sleeping Chesapeake Bay Retriever who had his big head in the small boy's lap. His grandfather sat down, reaching over to ruffle his grandson's hair as he smiled, surprised Blake was quiet.

"Johnny saw smoke and water rolling up over near Pea Island, and knew he was needing go check it out. It was August 16, 1918, a year after we entered the war, then another lookout reported a great mass of water shooting up in the air and saw the great ship continue her course for a few minutes, attempting to swing toward shore. Then mighty blasts of fire shot up from the stern and there were several heavy blasts after that.

"The sea was rough as they got the power boat and started out. It was difficult at first, and they had trouble getting her off the beach, but they tried four or five times, getting washed back each time, and finally cleared the beach in the afternoon. 'Bout five miles out, they could see the fire spreading across the water, sending up smoke and flames, obscuring the vision of the power boat heading in that direction. They met one of the ship's lifeboats coming out of the smoke, through a path that had not yet been consumed with fire. It carried the Captain and sixteen other men. The Captain told Johnny there were two other lifeboats, coming toward him, but he thought one had capsized, dumping all the men into the fiery sea. He said he thought all the men of that boat were burned to death."

Ellie gasped and put one hand on her heart and another to her mouth to suppress the emotion that welled up in her chest. Blake let out an inward breath gasp and Luke leaned forward, almost getting to his knees. Even the two Charlie's were awestruck. They knew the story but never heard the details of it like this.

Captain Levene continued, lost in the telling, "The captain of the stricken vessel said the name of his ship was the *Mirlo*, a British tanker, carrying gasoline and oil. Cap'n Johnny told the men of the *Mirlo*, to head for shore, but not to try to beach the boat, the sea would not allow it, get near the shore and wait, he would be back to get them in. He was going through the fire to get the others. Once again he stressed to the men of the *Mirlo* that they would not be able to maneuver the breakers near the shore without capsizing, and he was ordering them to wait for him. Sometimes it is difficult to take charge of another man's ship, but this was important, and he did not want to be overruled by the Captain of the *Mirlo*. Then, instructing his men to use a bucket to wet down the lifeboat, and themselves, he went into the burning scene before him.

"By this time the ship had broken in half, sending up double the smoke and fire in the air, and spreading gasoline across the sea, leaving a mass of fire on the water and two lifeboats somewhere in the middle. He saw, in between intervals of smoke clearing only briefly, stinging all their eyes, causing them to constantly blink to verify what they saw, there was one of the lifeboats bottom up, with men clinging to the sides, once in a while ducking under to avoid the flames which licked at them from the sea. Heavy sea swells kept washing over the both boats as the men struggled to stay alive.

Captain Johnny ran his boat in between flames to reach the men. Some of the men went under and never came back up. When Johnny reached the men, there were only six, all had burns, but were alive.

"Johnny ordered his men to keep dipping into the water when possible and keep themselves wet, as they were going through the fire again. The smell of smoke and gas was choking both victim and savior, but there was no time to stop, as the sub, according to the burned men, was still in the area, but sub or no sub, Johnny was going to try to save as many men as possible. The men pulled from the water did not know of the other boats. One of them had his skin burned almost all off, but he did not complain, he just allowed the Chicamacomico men to pull him in. They continued washing down the boat. Eventually all you could see were their eyes, they were all covered in soot. After he boarded the injured, Johnny went through the fire again, dodging wreckage and searching for the third boat. He found it with nineteen men aboard, so many men they could not row, and were helplessly drifting into and out of the burning water, as the wind directed them.

"Johnny threw a rope and taking the boat in tow, headed back toward the first lifeboat he had directed to shore. All boats were now charred from the fire which licked all around them. He reached the first boat, who had followed orders and waited. Now, towing a boat holding nineteen, with his crew and six burned victims, facing another boat to tow, Johnny realized he could not safely bring in two boats holding thirty-six lives. He took the wounded and directed both other boats to allow one of his men to board. The Rodanthe men knew better how to handle a boat in heavy seas. The sea was so violent, he loaded as many survivors as possible on the station boat and took them to the nearest shore.

"There the men from the other stations waited with horses and wagons to transport the men to the safe houses and to the station in Rodanthe. He went back three times to load his boat again, and trip by trip, he finally got them all to shore. His last trip was completed around nine o'clock at night. Once all the men from the *Mirlo* were safe he directed his crew to bring the lifeboats on shore. He finally got to his own head-quarters in Rodanthe (the Chicamacomico station) around 11:00pm. He saved forth-two lives that night. It was calculated that only nine were lost.

"On the shore, handling the horses and wagons were the men from the two nearby posts taking care of the wounded. At the Chicamacomico station, Miss Jazania, Johnny's wife, cooked more than 500 biscuits, plus clothed and applied medical aid to as much as was possible. She took care of and fed the crew of the *Mirlo*, every single man who helped in the rescue, all the men at the station and other stations on call that night, plus all the men who waited on shore to see to the needs of the stricken men. She even scolded the men from the *Mirlo* for chewing tobacco and spitting it on the floor. Quite a woman she was, a perfect match for Cap'n Johnny.

"It wern't till two years later did the world know of the deeds of Captain John Allen Midgett Jr. and his crew on that night. We were on strict orders to keep quiet about what was lurking in the sea around us, till the war was over. Twelve years later the men were awarded the Gold Life-Saving Medal for gallantry by our nation and the Silver Cup by the British Trade Commission, also with our countries' greatest tribute the Grand Cross of the American Cross of Honor."

MIRLO RESCUE TEAM

John Allen Midgett Jr.
Clarence E. Midgett
Arthur Midgett
Zion Midgett
Leroy Midgett
Prochorus O'Neal (brother-in-law of John Allen Midgett Jr.)

World War I ended November 11, 1918.

On the ride back home, the kids slept. The day had been long, and the breeze from the ocean wafted through the windows across their faces. As they fought to keep their eyes open, the familiar rumble over the camel-backs made by the incoming and receding tide was gently rocking them to sleep. For them it had been an eventful day, they had paid close attention, and lived through Cap'n Levene's story as it happened. In their minds, they had seen the drama, and now, as they relaxed, sleep came quickly.

Cap'n Charlie and his friend Charlie Williams from Kinnakeet just talked. They too had experienced an eventful day, which for both older men had started early. They had learned much that day and had the burden of what had been decided by the other elders of the island on how to proceed forward in their continued fight in this war. Their objective was to protect the innocent villagers and provide help to the government men who had come to the island to keep them from danger.

The two men were aware that as night fell, there would be multiple attacks, as there were every night. There would be men struggling to come to shore from a sinking ship and facing the possibility of being strafed by the deck guns of the enemy. As a result, most would die before reaching land. Others would make it in boats leaking from the gunshot holes, near death, shot, burned, injured, scared, and lucky to get to this island, where everyone, man or woman, was willing to give whatever they had, which was not much, to see that the survivors returned to their own homes.

With this in mind, two of the most important men of the island could not help but look to the sea. They felt they were being watched even though they saw only a black sea, the enemy was out there, lurking under the blue black ocean, which reflected the moon as it rose in the horizon, and they knew, it was only a matter of time before the horrible destruction would begin again. The war was still there, all the villagers knew it; the men in the car with sleeping children knew it. There was still much work to do.

★ 10 ★

They Were Valiant

And when they seek to oppress you,
And when they try to destroy you,
Rise and rise again and again,
Like the Phoenix from the ashes.
Until the lambs have become lions,
and the rule of Darkness is no more.

MAITREYA The Friend of all Souls,
The Holy Book of Destiny (Hindu)

Easter vacation was coming to a close. The children had had an exciting few days off. Their exploration of the caves and their visit to the Chicamacomico station and Cap'n Levene was probably more excitement than any other three children had had during that ten day holiday. Some of it they could tell, and some of it they could not, but they had each other, and as the excitement of Easter Sunday approached, they spent the time resting and reminiscing about all the things they had seen and done. They huddled in Blake's closet and rehashed the entire visit to the cave, and what they had seen on the beach as they drove on the wash from Buxton to Rodanthe.

The war was still going on, and on Saturday night before what was an anticipated wonderful arrival of the Easter Bunny for Blake, and an Easter surprise in the morning, the U-Boats struck again, and the houses shook, awaking everyone all up and down the southern shore of Hatteras Island, causing men to rise from their beds, women help them prepare by seeing they were fed, as the unsettling horror of what others were experiencing disturbed their sleepless night and morning.

Easter morning did arrive, with a sleepy group of grown-ups, and a less than excited group of children gathered in front of the fireplace to explore what the bunny had managed to gather together for three baskets. There was not much candy, as rationing was in place, but there were small toys, colored eggs and sweets hidden among pretty crocheted flowers, from Grandmom, and shredded colored crepe paper together with Christmas tensile and left-over Christmas "snow" which lined the baskets. Grandmom had also given each child a beautiful small red velvet bag, with a gold rope pull to close it shut. The boys held theirs up and looked at it strangely.

"What's this for?" asked Blake, as he stuck his finger in it, and found it empty.

Ellie gave Grandmom a knowing wink, she knew.

"Oh, I saw them at the store when I was there, they were in a glass case. I just thought you might have a use for them.", answered Grandmom.

"I have a small treasure which will be perfect in this," said Ellie as she looked at both of the boys.

The boys were silent. *How did Grandmom know?* they thought.

When they got to their rooms, they pulled out the treasures from the cave and each placed them in the velvet bag and pulled it closed.

Grandmom and Nett had done their best, and all put on a brave face in hopes of staving off tears, as joy was marred by reality.

Grandpop, through his tired face bravely reminded the children, and maybe even Grandmom and Nett, that this was a special day, a day when hope was celebrated, and the promise of sunny skies and pretty new flowers was on the horizon. Sometimes we have to wait for things, he had said, and everyone understood. That morning the milk tasted sweeter, the pancakes had drizzles of honey, and they all managed to be happy about something.

After breakfast, they all raced to their rooms to put on their finest new clothes, and admire what they had, rather than what they did not. Ellie was the most appreciative, as she knew one of her best friends, whose parents had also died, and who, like Ellie, lived with her Grandfather, would be there, not in new clothes, with probably no Easter basket, and only one penny for collection. She reached in her drawer and pulled out a pretty ribbon and a box she had been saving. In it she put one of the pearls she had found in the cave, inside a crocheted flower (Grandmom vowed she would replace it for Ellie) and rested it on some of the shredded crepe paper, silver tensile and cotton Christmas snow from her basket, also she added two colored eggs, and all of the candy from her basket. She would eat from Blake and Luke's basket. The story would be that this was a gift left at her house, for Agnes, from the Easter Bunny.

Grandpop had surprised Grandmom with a new frock and a beautiful flowered hat, from the best ladies' shop in Manteo. Everyone got new clothes for Easter. Ellie had a new dress made, with ribbons to match. As a special surprise, she got new patent leather Mary Jane shoes, and ruffled socks, like the other girls wore. No more ugly ankle boots, to protect her weak ankles, as they were no longer weak, but stronger, since her health had improved with Weroansquoa's visit. She was so excited she could not stop looking at them and danced around the room like she was on stage.

Even the boys got new suits from the Sears and Roebuck catalog, and Nett also sported a new dress and hat, from the catalog. The day was picking up, as they sang "Jesus Loves Me" all the way to church in the car. Grandpop was glad when the car drove up to the church yard. He almost sprinted over to the other men waiting outside the church in their familiar groups to chat. As tired as he was, the children were driving him crazy. The day was beautiful, birds were just flitting around the trees like they had something to say. There was a breeze from the ocean, though once in a while, a whiff of oil came through, but things on the hill were as good as could be. The children changed clothes and went to the barn, still, it was Sunday, and no matter the occasion, there was to be little noise on that day.

Grandmom cooked up the ham Grandpop had purchased from a neighbor who had slaughtered a few for the village. She had even made potato salad, and stewed apples from her canning selection on the porch. This day they had a cake made with fruit cocktail and nuts topped with tasty cream from Twinkle. It was a very happy Easter Sunday, and Grandpop, full from the bread Grandmom had baked, retired to the chair in his study to sleep away the entire afternoon.

The war hardly took a breath.

The remains of ships and lifeboats were strewn across the sands between villages. The villagers maintained a steady task of removing from the beaches the awful reminders. It appeared to be never-ending. Daily, the people of the communities tried to clean the beach, only to find more debris from new battles at sea once again resting in the now discolored sand.

Grooming the hooves of the horses was also a constant job, the tar and oil washing up from the torpedoed ships made its way through the tides and deposited itself on the shore, and, with the same consistency that formerly allowed the lacy foam to collect and fade as it rushed back to the pristine ocean. No more, this mess was too heavy to wash back. It was apparent when children disobeyed their parents and went to the beach, because there was so much tar they could not escape the tell-tale sign of their disregard. Life had changed drastically and there seemed to be no end. Villagers were quietly dealing with their plight, while on the mainland, others, both men and now women, who were unaware of what was going on off their shores, were busy taking jobs they had never experienced before, working in the war factories of the United States. We had not come to this war unprepared. Since after our lack of readiness caught us off guard during World War I, we knew we could never again consider ourselves detached from other nations. We needed to anticipate that war was inevitably going to involve us, no matter where in the world it was. The sea surrounding us was no longer a barrier. It could and was being broached.

Our youth was leaving for the war effort in droves. Even they did not know what was happening at home. The parents left behind in their villages knew the danger of revealing the truth. The newspapers were silent, reporters were banned; the island was again isolated from the rest of the United States, not by choice but by government order. It would have created a panic of epic proportions had the average citizen known what was lurking in the waters off their coast. The war effort by Americans was massive. Still, we did not produce fast enough to provide convoys for the endangered ships or planes to patrol the air over the coast. Keeping quiet was the best defense older villagers could provide for their young, who fought on two fronts, and also here at home.

Some from the island were stationed in the Pacific, where the mighty war machine of Japanese ships and planes sought to destroy the islands and make their way to the western shores of the United States. Our boys fought them in the islands of the Pacific and in the air over other islands taken over by the enemy. We were also on the ground and in the air in Europe, desperately holding off the Germans, while this country was doing everything they could at home to keep the war away. Americans were dying all over the world. For the enemy, the war was in two parts, the Axis powers of Western Europe combined with the country of Japan in the east, both with hopes of meeting in the middle, and then dividing up the world. It was not called a World War for nothing. No country was safe, the Germans were also on the continent of Africa, the Japanese headed for Australia and New Zealand, destroyed the islands of the Pacific, invaded the countries of mainland China, Korea and Indo-China, hoping to finish them off and land on the Pacific shores of California, and South America.

South America was also trying to keep the war contained, as they mined ore, and farmed rubber from the trees to provide tires, sent oil and gasoline from their fields, cultivated food stuffs for Europe, copper from the countries of Chile and Peru, tin from Bolivia, coffee from Columbia, also lumber from most countries of South America combined with fuel from the state of Louisiana's gulf coast and grain from Mississippi. All of this was on transport ships headed for Europe, by way of the shores of the Atlantic, and using the ocean river called the Gulf Stream that flowed past and curved off to Europe. This was the "gold mine" the Germans sought to destroy.

Captain Charlie had five sons in the war, six counting Bill Finnegan, two in the navy, two in the coast guard, one a merchant marine, on one of those transports threatened by German U-boats, and Bill in the navy. His was the story of the island, in the villages of Buxton, Kinnakeet, Hatteras, Trent, Waves, Salvo and Rodanthe, all families had friends and relatives overseas. This island was one who served. It was up to the older generation, and the wives and sisters left at home to protect the country as best they could in the war effort.

Inside the United States, on the mainland, the country worked in factories who had turned their peacetime production into industries supplying materials for war: planes, ships, tanks, heavy trucks, guns and ammunition, bombs, anything to help the Allied countries of Europe to beat back the intruders. It was an all-out effort.

As Captain Charlie and Charlie Williams rode back home by way of low tide on the shore of the Atlantic, they heard the roar of a ship, and with binoculars saw the lonely patrol of our only destroyer, the USS

Roper, and, looking north and south, also they observed the silhouettes of local fishing vessels, who were patrolling where they could.

The Germans sometimes referred to their U-boat activity as "The Wolfpack". They patrolled in twos. Three or more subs were permanently located at Diamond Shoals, resting on the bottom at day, then attacking and patrolling at night. They were involved in "Operation Paukenschlag (Drumbeat)." Hitler wanted to punish the Americans for their convoys of war materials and food, to his enemies. He wanted to strike a blow as jarring as a drum beating. When they were able to sink many Allied ships, they named it their "Happy Time". The area once known as the Hatteras Graveyard, and the Graveyard of the Atlantic, was now also referred to as "Torpedo Junction."

When the island turned off its lights, and the lighthouse went dark, the enemy rowed to shore in the dead of night and set fire to the sea grass so they could use it as a back-drop to spot ships going by in the dark. There were so many bodies washed up on shore near the southern point of Nags Head they named the lighthouse there, Bodie Island Light. The carnage created by German U-boats caused a news blackout of Hatteras Island. Hitler wanted to create another Pearl Harbor, so he immediately sent five U-boats to American coast, and increased to twelve then to nineteen. This was now referred to as "The Great American Turkey Shoot."

The first ship blown up near the Cape Hatteras shore was the *Dixie Arrow*. Its occupants jumped into the burning sea of oil, as Helmsman Oscar Chappell burned to death trying to steer the ship out of harm's way. He was trying to get the ship out of the oil and reverse the wind to keep the fire at bay. In doing so the wind directed the fire on him, as others jumped into the untainted water. While his men tried to save themselves, the third torpedo fired directly into the pilothouse. Chappell died at the helm.

Sharks were also a problem and the decision was sometimes to stay and be blown up or jump and be eaten up. The destroyer USS *Tarbell* dropped depth charges in the area knocking some survivors unconscious, and seeing those struggling to survive, the USS *Tarbell* stopped and picked up as many as possible and took them out of harm's way. The Coast Guard also arrived on the scene as quickly as possible but were careful, as the sub had waited around to destroy the escaping survivors. Over the next six months, many, many lifeboats came to shore, empty of souls and full of holes.

Subs even blinked lights to give false information and draw ships to them. So many ships were blown out of the water, the living drifted among the bloated bodies hoping to survive and get to shore. Grossadmiral Karl Donitz was commander of the U-Boats in the area. His goal was to sink 700,000 tons of supplies a month. He felt the Americans were both inexperienced, and mostly unprotected. The shoals off Cape Hatteras forced the ships to the edge of deep water, where the subs waited. There was only one large cutter left to patrol 28,000, miles off the Carolinas and near the harbors of Virginia. The Germans eventually mined the Virginia harbors, and set underwater steel nets across the channels.

The Navy and Coast Guard worked together feverishly to control the undefended shores of North Carolina. The Germans were looking to sink tankers of 10,000 pounds plus, and any commander who destroyed 100,000 pounds won the Knight's Cross. This was the prize they all wanted. Once attaining that goal, they returned to Germany as "rock stars", to pick up more torpedoes and get back to work. Operation Drumbeat sank five ships in four days. The Germans had so many targets they had to pick and choose for tonnage. On one "night of the long knives," they beat the drum honoring the sinking of eight ships.

Meanwhile, it had happened so fast, war declared on December 11, 1941, and less than one month later, by January of 1942, the killers were off the shores of this island, and sank five ships in four days. In the month of January, they sank forty ships, costing more than five hundred lives. The island was not dark, the lighthouse was still burning, radio silence was not yet implemented, and school students were hearing the blasts as they walked to school. According to Gibb Gray, a young man on his way to school in Kinnakeet, he looked in the direction of the sea and saw the entire sky red.

The walls of the island houses cracked, cisterns for collecting rainwater for drinking and washing clothes sprang leaks from the long fissures going up their sides. Windows rattled, some blew inward, and the rumble of noise went through the water and up the dunes to vibrate under the feet of the villagers. In Kinnakeet, the reverberation was felt under the classroom seats, as the teacher yelled, "RUN!" As they did run, the walls around them buckled.

U.S. Rear Admiral Adolphus Andrews begged for help. He needed escorts for ships, and planes to patrol and drop bombs on surfaced subs, in all, protection. He was told there was none, all their ships and planes were somewhere else, either in the Atlantic, on the shores of Europe, or in the Pacific. Hatteras Island was on its own!

The United States had turned every peacetime factory into one for war materials. Women who had never worked before, went to work manufacturing screws, or bolts, or parts for a ship or plane. Every able-bodied adult on the mainland was working as hard as possible to produce what was needed for the war we fought on two fronts, both the Atlantic and the Pacific. There were two killers, Germany and Japan, worlds apart, but both in close proximity of the United States.

The Navy warned mariners to protect themselves; run their boats without lights, stay in shallow water, and go past the Graveyard of the Atlantic only in daylight. Ships heard screaming as they sank, men trapped under decks working on engines, or blocked by the crumbling steel that kept them from escaping. Locals saw lifeboats come ashore empty. Kids found them as they left the school building and, like kids, sneaked to the beach to see what they could see. There, finding empty lifeboats, they looked for rations, and gear hidden under the seats, possibly chocolate or jars of malted milk tablets.

The beginning of the war was marked by chaos. Then the bodies began to appear on the beach, and everything changed for the innocent. Gibb Gray described what he saw from the dunes that day the *Dixie Arrow* was blown out of the sea. The Coast Guard had launched toward the sea, now black in places, filled with so much smoke the ship kept disappearing from view, then as the wind blew, it lifted the smoke for an instant, he even saw occupants of the tanker jump into the burning water heavy with oil, and vanish. Oil tankers burned for days and more than fifty years later one could see isolated ribbons of beautiful colors streaking the waters of Diamond Shoals. The island was then put on notice, no lights at night, use blankets or heavy dark shades on the windows, use of flashlights was prohibited, as the lighthouse went dark.

The passenger/cargo ship *City of New York*, 8,272 tons, with a cargo of 6612 tons of chrome ore, wood, wool, hides and asbestos, the first ship of the American-South American line, was the next victim. The unescorted ship was hit by two torpedoes from U-#160 while moving through raging twenty foot seas fifty miles east of Cape Hatteras. The ship's armed guards fired back from the ship's deck guns, with no positive results. Some of the 144 passengers and crew boarded four lifeboats, only to spend days in the frozen water, while the fifth sank and burned. One passenger birthed a baby, Jesse Roper Mohorovicic, named after the *USS Jesse Roper*, which finally picked them out of the sea. The doctor, from another lifeboat which tied on, delivered the baby in spite of his two broken ribs. The frozen passengers did what they could to save mother and child. It was days before the other lifeboats were located by the *USS Roper*, still the seas were often fifteen feet high.

During two weeks in March, twenty-one ships were hit, and the average rose first to be at least one a day, then to more. The German Johann Moore took out several ships in six hours in 260ft. water. Islanders began to act, covering headlights and windows. Some painted their headlights black with only one or two inches of light to see. Admiral

Andrews continued to petition for assistance of planes and destroyers but was denied. For months *the USS Roper* was the only destroyer to assist the U.S. off the coast of Cape Hatteras. Ships would drop lifeboats full of survivors, merely to have them connect with burning oil on the water and incinerate the victims. Ships accidentally fired on other ships mistaking them for U-boats, only to reveal themselves and be sunk by a waiting German submarine. The entire scene was chaos, as the Navy gave out less and less information to the mainland to cover up what was going on within miles of their shores. Villagers were constantly attempting to remove and hide the carnage on their doorsteps.

Islanders kept constant vigil over the beaches, checking every day for signs of life, whose nationality did not matter, life and death became a daily struggle. Local men and women signed up to be coastal watchers. Captain Charlie, and Maude White, the postmistress, were among them. Islanders found German rafts in the bushes and dunes and began to be suspicious of anyone they considered a stranger. Everyone on the island was forbidden to go to the beach. The cement bunker near the lighthouse, which the children had found while playing was now occupied every hour of the day and night. Sometimes victims washed up on the shore after having been in the water for a month. The locals buried all they found, giving a proper burial to all, as time allowed.

Miss Maude, the post mistress checked parcels being mailed from the post office. To her, some sailors were also strangers, therefore she checked everything and everyone. Once, a stranger speaking perfect English attempted to mail an especially heavy package, and as she questioned the weight, he said they were books. After the stranger left, her daughter, Carol, sitting in the building with her, reminded her that the island did not sell books. Maude White, coastal watcher and postmistress notified the FBI who intercepted the package. It contained mapping of the shore from South Carolina through North Carolina. The FBI began their search, now on alert to the additional area of danger. A foreign couple was detained after getting off the ferry, but it was not clear if they were the ones. Word spread through the island and they became even more cautious of what was possible. Suspicion grew.

The U-boats having arrived only six weeks after Pearl Harbor were war boats, and spent most of their time above water, as they could only submerge for limited periods of time. They were 219 feet long and could travel at thirty mph, and could run sixty miles before having to surface, carried fifty men, fifteen torpedoes, which after spent, sent them back to Germany for more. This did not deter the numbers as those leaving were replaced by other U-boats, in a rotation system. These were killing grounds.

Most Americans were unaware of how bad things were, as the Naval Security teams checked all communications to hide the truth from the mainland, while they fought in every way, they could to change the outcome.

The islanders were living in a war zone, just skirting the edges of danger, being exposed to danger, looking at it, testing it, but respectful of it. They put themselves at risk each day and night and considered it their duty to do so. The same bravery and selflessness that lived in the surfmen, also lived in the hearts of the ordinary islanders. They were determined to fight the war at home while their sons and daughters fought it in foreign lands. They followed those around who did not speak the island tongue, this became almost a game to the children, who defied danger, as did their parents. They would report at supper who and what they had seen on the island. This was keeping them from the beach, and swimming, and loading their sand with ugly tar, and they were not happy about it. Parents were constantly worried at what their children were doing, but were themselves so busy with the bigger aspect, policing the children added to the already daunting problem.

Private fishing vessels and their local captains were among the bravest, as they also patrolled for U-boats. They considered it harassment to an enemy they could not kill and were fearless and mighty proud to be a part. Their efforts were admirable, but only a pin-prick or a nuisance to the Germans, who, also admired the tenacity of the locals. In their human hearts, they hoped their loved ones left at home were of the same ilk. Meanwhile the enemy was so close to their victims they listened to the crooning of Bing Crosby, and the music of Guy Lombardo and Harry James on their short-wave radio.

As the non-combatants joined the effort, they were unaware of the orders to the submarines that tonnage was important, and the U-boats were continuing to try to avoid tangling with the local detractors, knowing they could not afford to use one of the limited torpedoes on a three man fishing boat. The bravery and national pride of the island was infectious. Spies on the island were a known fact, and many suspects were apprehended for as long a period of time as it took for them to be checked out by the FBI, some who exhibited suspicion were detained needlessly, but detained they were.

As homes and buildings shook and walls cracked, the locals always compared notes, they remarked to each other about feeling it, touching it, hearing it, smelling it and all that brought the communities closer. Some even volunteered to help with grooming of the new horses in the corrals in Kinnakeet. Those new riders were inexperienced young men from all over the United States, mostly Texas, and were scared themselves, also ready to shoot anything that they saw, especially at night, even when it was just a shadow. The island was full of what the islanders called "strangers". Some were those young men new to the Coast Guard, but they still made the locals nervous.

Also, volunteering were Yachting clubs, who had gotten wind of what was happening while on their regular fishing trips to the island, even knowing the risk, and the need for secrecy, they still wanted to be a part of the Navy but were too old to be inducted. They came from everywhere, but as they moved about the island, they too became a part of the group called strangers, by the community. The Cruising Club of America, made up of seventy yachts, presented themselves for service, as well as the

Hooligan Navy. These men were used in their capacity as coastal watchers, but with a better vantage point, and as they harassed the submarines with their presence, they could also radio back suspicious positions when there was an unusual disturbance in the water. Each volunteer was sworn to secrecy as to what was happening on the eastern island off the coast of the United States. Again, "loose lips, sink ships". These off-island men were proud to keep their mouths shut and their eyes open, for the amount of time they were involved. Nothing leaked, nothing!

Ocracoke Island had an anti-submarine patrol basin and hid the structures in the dunes and beyond. Being stationed on one of these islands was not a pleasant duty, finding out one was being transferred to an island was at first looked on as a lucky assignment, palm trees waving, crystal blue seas, beautiful young girls, ready to dance with them in the moonlight. But they were disappointed to find there were no dances, just mosquitoes and biting green flies, hot sand and suspicious locals. Also, the loneliness of nothing to do added to the distance and prohibition of liberty on the mainland. The thought that they would consume enough alcohol to blab something secret to others was scary to the powers that controlled the security of this situation. On Ocracoke, the local ladies helped when they could, by doing laundry for the sailors when the cisterns went dry, or maybe having them over for a home cooked meal, and eventually, some fell in love with local girls and forgot the hardships of the isolation and boredom of the island, as opposed to the city they came from. Many stayed beyond the war to become a part of that they did not at first appreciate. They at first, even chastised the islanders for always being barefoot, until they found how irritating the sand could be in a closed shoe, then everyone shed shoes whenever possible. But, for some, the depression and disappointment of what they did not see of "action", and "the world", was too much, and they took measures to get away, some purposefully injured themselves hoping for a mainland hospital, only to be quarantined in a place where they could be monitored.

The islanders could hear the sound of the German sub off shore, surfacing under cover of darkness, as it recharged its batteries. The subs made a low humming sound, as it went across the water, and locals could actually feel the hum under their feet, as it reverberated through the sand. They could put their hand to the ground and know what was coming. It was the sound of death in preparation. As ships sank, the island shook from dropped depth charges, which resonated across the land. Those who went to the windows facing the ocean saw fire shooting up one hundred feet or more. There was still no protection for the merchant victims of the drumroll. The U-boats had taken the "human" out of the war, there was no fight, just destruction. Constant depth charges from merchant ships hoping to fight back sent both heart pounding pulsations and expectations for those hearing it on shore, and for those on ships listening and watching for debris to surface, they anticipated maybe they got the undersea monster stalking them. Again, it had to be a perfect hit, or crushing explosions on either side of the sub, to do any damage. The odds were against the victim being stalked on the surface.

Captain Bill Gaskell from Ocracoke sent his son to war on a merchant ship named the *Caribsea*. He worried because never heard from him again. U-boat #158, with Captain Erwin Rostin chasing tonnage of a tanker off the coast of Cape Lookout lighthouse, caught the shadow of the *Caribsea*, and as it appeared larger than it was, Rostin left the tanker and aimed for what he thought was a Coast Guard vessel, stopped, and possibly looking for him. The Captain of the *Caribsea* had slowed his engines to try and pass the Cape Hatteras lighthouse in daylight and was torpedoed as it waited in shallow waters. Hit in the boiler room, it sank in less than three minutes, sending out no distress signal, and giving no time to launch lifeboats. Only a few survivors climbed into two rafts that had floated free as they observed the U-boat passing within 100 yards. They used a tin can to catch the sun and reflect as a signal, until they finally floated clear of the explosion area.

Later that week, still no news from his son, Jim Baughm, the old man, Cap'n Bill, was bothered by a large plank-like oar constantly hitting the dock where he would launch his small boat, he reached down, and using his rake, dragged the obstacle from the water. On the plank was the nameplate of the *Caribsea*. He knew the fate his son had suffered. The nameplate later was made into part of a cross, which stood at the altar of Gaskill's church on Ocracoke island.

Another sailor whose ship had been torpedoed, swam back to the sinking ship, made his way through the twisted metal and distorted hallways to his quarters, pulled out the American flag from his locker and breathing where he could as the ship sank, he hoisted it to the top most point he could make his way to, and as another torpedo slammed into the ship. While the ship sank, the rescue ship drew near, but all the approaching sailors could see was the American flag, and the ship as it slid under the water also showing the railing of the bow, with the name *Naeco*.

By April 1942, there were nineteen U-boats operating off the coast of Cape Hatteras. The slaughter was sometimes marked by lifeboats which got caught in the davits, making them unable to launch, or ones destroyed by the fire from the gasoline and oil which burned the ship to submission.

> *"The only thing that ever really frightened*
> *me during the war was the U-boat peril."*
> WINSTON CHURCHILL

Often sailors jumped overboard to pull in survivors from decks so hot it melted their shoes. They tried to judge where the fire would float and jumped where it had not hit, underwater, they grabbed someone they saw and helped them in their panic, and tried to bring them up with them. Survival was brutal, but managed at all costs, they came up for air when they saw a blue spot above them and again went under when the fire spread.

In occupied France, the French Resistance knew how much the American military was helping, and they knew the cost. Many of the women innocently watched from the shoreline to pass word of submarine departure on to resistance channels in London. They were aware that if the subs were leaving, they would show up on American shores. Any chamber maids or dock workers who knew about departures, passed along the information. They did not know the destination, but it could only be America.

The German sailors, after a while heard of the hardships of serving underwater, the stench, rotting food, smell of diesel oil, human sweat, urine, musty clothing, cooking odors, as every square inch of that underwater vessel was filled with provisions. Sometimes the air inside the submarines got overloaded with carbon dioxide, and it made the men tired, and caused them stink. It was not the glorious life of bravery they had been led to believe.

Constantly, they listened for pings from the radar above to let them know to avoid a depth charge, as it got louder, they knew to the man it was near, and they had been discovered. The sailors sweat as they looked toward the ceiling waiting and waiting, listening to the charges being dropped closer and closer, sometimes it hit close but not *on*, leaks began to spring as charges came faster, fire consumed the quarters of the can of men, as they broke out hoses to quell the inevitable, and after a safe while, they needed to surface and access the damage. The first to die were those in the engine room, and that also became knowledgeable to those making the voyage.

It was during those times of waiting that they dared to surface, they needed fresh air and a bath in the sea. If lucky, they surfaced in an area with no sharks, but their very person drew the other hunters of the sea, and their liberty was cut short. Watching the kids became their most enjoyable pastime, and quite a distance out to sea, they carefully watched and dreamed of horses, dogs and children left at home.

Finally, the destroyer, *USS Roper* detected and sank German U-#85, off the outer banks between Wimble Shoals (located off Rodanthe's coast) and Cape Hatteras banks. They realized it housed one of the famous *Enigma* machines, a machine that could deciphered code from nations attempting to send messages that could only be read by the intended recipient. For weeks naval divers attempted to recover the valuable machine, to no avail. The only conciliation was that this one would no longer be in use. This was physical proof that there was more to war than fire and destruction. Knowledge was paramount in winning.

The war as it was fought off the coast of the island of Cape Hatteras was as sophisticated and horrible as any fought on any island of the Pacific. This was the island of choice by the German Third Reich. The resolute villagers of the island proved their metal as they put their own lives aside, faced the peril, and helped save the United States and her Allies. Although these facts were kept secret from the mainland, and the islanders knew it, it made no difference. They did not feel courageous, nor were they afraid. They were asked to do a job and they did it to the best of their ability and with the tools they had at their disposal. Most of what they offered was bravery and selflessness. They were valiant men.

A few of the supply ships who were lost off this coast and the U-boats who destroyed them:

Known names of the U-boats sent to the area during the war:

RIO BLANCO	U-85
TIGER	U-352
SPLENDOUR	U-701
BYRON T BENSON	U-567
HARRY F. SINCLAIR JR	U-71
SAN DELFINO	U-656
HARPAGON	U-160
ALCOA GUIDE	U-158
SAN JACINTO	U-576
MALAY	
ALLEN JACKSON	
EMPIRE GEM	
KASSANDRA	
ACME	
BUARQUE	
LOULOUDIS	
DIXIE ARROW	
LIGHTHOUSE SHIP #71	
CITY OF NEW YORK	
CARIBSEA	
BLUEFIELS	
CITY OF ATLANTA	

These are only a fraction of the ships torpedoed off the coast of Cape Hatteras, and only a few of the German submarines who were responsible. It was a killing field of rare intensity. It lasted six months.

⋆ 11 ⋆

The War Is Over

Thou unknown hero sleeping by the sea
In thy forgotten grave! With secret shame
I feel my pulses beat, my forehead burn,
When I remember thou hast given for me
All that thou hadst, thy life, thy very name,
And I can give thee nothing in return.

A Nameless Grave,
Henry Wadsworth Longfellow

Spring was on the island. The cool breezes off the ocean were sometimes clean, sometimes not, but the sea was trying to lift the spirits of
all who were near.

It was Mother's Day. The Gray family went to church early, Pop was
the Sunday school teacher for the adult men, and Nett needed to help
the other young ladies decorate the church in honor of all the mothers
of the village. The children did not mind getting to the white clapboard
Methodist church early, they too were on a mission. They knew where

to find the best roses. Uncle Alaska and Aunt Minnie had two white German shepherd dogs, and a yard full of roses of all colors, and, they lived only three houses from the church. Luke and Blake were going for the prettiest red roses to wear in honor of their mother, and Ellie was excited about finding two roses. One white for her mother Annie, who had died giving birth to her, and the biggest, reddest, most gorgeous rose to show her love for her grandmother, Odessa, who was the only mother she had ever known. She also picked two other white ones for her Grandfather and Grandmother to wear in memory of their parents. Luke and Blake also picked another red rose for their mother to wear. By the time they ended, Aunt Minnie had to get them a basket for the number of beautiful blooms they had. The old couple also had the most wonderful Mother's Day, as they were pleased to have been visited by Odessa's sweet grandchildren on this day. Having no children, Aunt Minnie was thrilled.

Roses for the day were not the only reason the kids enjoyed visiting their great-aunt and uncle, they got to play with those handsome white German shepherd dogs. They were so fluffy and friendly, almost as tall as the kids, but lovable. One of them was blind, and Ellie loved him the most. She would put her head against him, and tell him all that she saw, and fill him with hugs and squeezes until Aunt Minnie was afraid maybe the poor old thing would bite Odessa's child. The shepherds knew Ellie better than Aunt Minnie did, absence of presence did not mean absence of connection. These dogs knew no other person like they did Ellie, no matter how few times they were in her company. The blind dog lived for communicating with the pretty little girl. They were friends, and the animal understood everything Ellie said, and she him. His name was Snow, and his brother's name was Wind, and they both had a special bond with Ellie. Of course, the boys played with them also, but it was not the same as talking to them, like Ellie did. All the children of the families loved the old couple and visited them whenever they could. Aunt Minnie was quite the baker.

Uncle Alaska was a retired Lighthouse keeper in Rock Point, Maryland, where he met and befriended General Billy Mitchell, who, on Alaska's invitation followed him to the island, to see if the hunting was as good as he had been told. Mitchell later proved his theory about the use of planes in wartime by sinking ships from his plane off the coast of the village of Hatteras. Billy also met several friends of Alaska's who had duck blinds located in the Pamlico Sound, and they enjoyed many hours together hunting. At night, after a day on the water, they played cards with the Hatteras men who shared their duck blinds. They usually played down at the Atlantic View motel, with the Austin boys and others. He was just Billy and became a fixture to the locals. Everyone knew Billy Mitchell. The two men kept in touch, however Mitchell did not live to see his theory in action. Uncle Alaska always said he expected Billy would be responsible for winning the war for the United States. He was correct, as planes proved to play a massive part for both sides.

Blake's idol was Billy Mitchell, and he was almost a nuisance to Uncle Alaska, as he pestered him about the General, until Luke made him shut up. Blake, however, was no bother to his great-uncle, who loved him as if he was his own grandson. As a young man, Alaska and his younger sister Odessa, were the only ones to explore the stone mansion in Trent Woods, which they knew belonged in the Jennette family. After he retired and moved home, he and his wife, Minnie visited his sister Odessa and her husband often after they moved to Trent Woods, and the two siblings giggled like kids when they sat on the porch and remembered their clandestine excursions through the house. Blake wondered if they had discovered the secret floor with all the trunks, but he was afraid to ask just in case he was wrong and would then have to explain himself.

There were two other Jennette brothers, Utah and Unaka. They were both lighthouse keepers, one at Cape Henry (Fort Story) in Virginia Beach, Virginia, and another for a time at Cape Hatteras. It was a happy time when the three brothers got together; they had so much in common.

Only Alaska had an inkling of the unusual powers born to the women of the Jennette family. He watched as his sister exhibited her intuition when near the house in Trent Woods. Odessa had the powers but chose not to use them. She had been told in a dream that her job was to foster those same powers in one of her daughters. She had first noticed specialness in her youngest daughter, Annie, but Annie's strength was not strong enough to accept the challenge. She died giving birth to a little girl and evidently passed on some of her frailties to her daughter, Ellie. One weakness was apparent when it displayed itself each time she was faced with an injury, either a cut or a bruise. At that point she exhibited a complication that prevented her blood from clotting.

Ellie was handled gingerly as a child and young girl growing up. Everyone was afraid that she would bleed to death when cut. This made her special to the wolves, and they protected her. As she grew, her strength of mind and body grew also. Grandmom began to detect that this was the exceptional child she had dreamed about, as she observed the way the animals responded to her. Watching Ellie, and her connection to his dogs, Uncle Alaska also suspected the same.

On this fine spring day, with the thought of a mother's love filling up the empty spaces left by the fear of loss, Grandpop and Grandmom, with her brother and sister-in law, sat on the long porch of the stone house and listened to the sounds of the breeze blowing through the woods and the twitter of birds who did not know, nor fear the trouble at sea. Nett had made a special dinner for them all, in honor of Mother's Day, and was inside getting ready to serve dessert and tea to her guests. To all of their surprise, the sound of a plane engine split the silence of the afternoon, as they, almost in unison, rose from their rockers and stepped out to the edge of the porch and scanned the sky to see if it actually was what they imagined it to be. Sure enough, there was a search plane in the air over the ocean. Could it be that help had finally arrived? Cap'n Charlie and Alaska looked at each other with questioning expressions that immediately changed to huge grins. They shook hands and said *Finally!* The women hugged, it meant so much to them. Hope filled everyone. Hope for them, hope for their loved ones, it seemed to have been so long since they had felt that feeling.

Also, hearing the plane were the three kids, who were in the barn grooming their horses. They ran outside and looked up and saw the unfamiliar sight. They knew the importance of the plane, they had heard enough to know that everyone was always saying, "if only there was air support," the U-boats would not be able to be so successful. The children knew they were not supposed to listen to any conversation among the adults. They couldn't help it, so they just acted like they were not paying attention, while the whole time, kicking each other under the table, or giving that knowing side eye of recognition. This sight had them jumping up and down. They ran to the porch, in a race, of course.

Blake got there first, Luke saw to that, "Can we take the horses on the beach? All of them. Please, please, nothing can happen to us today! Could we please? We'll take care of Ol' Tony and Big Roy, they will follow us. Luke and I will hold one each, they haven't had a good run or bath forever, you know they will not leave the other horses. Horses always stay in a herd. Please?" He was out of breath, but determined to be heard.

Grandpop, still with a grin on his face, gave permission, not to do so would have spoiled an afternoon with the family. Moping kids always put a damper on the day, although, these kids almost knew when the answer would be 'no' and avoided the question.

They raced once again to the barn. This time Ellie, last man to the porch, had a head start and got to Blue before the others. Throwing on the blankets and getting astride with leads on the two surf horses, they headed out the back path through the trees and bushes to the sea. It had been so long since they had taken this path,. Now that spring was almost closing it in, they knew they also needed to clear it, but that would not be done today. It would be a later date, not Sunday, but after school or

Saturday. Now, they would just muscle their way through. Poor Pegasus, it was his job to break the way, but Ol' Tony also helped as he went beside Pegasus as a partner. In their minds they wanted the horses to get a run and some air, and to wade in the water. They decided on the way that they would keep a sharp eye out for the dolphin. They did have the feeling it would be a futile effort, as it was too soon; just one plane did not solve everything, but here again, there was hope.

By the end of May, the United States and Great Britain had gathered together enough vessels of various kinds to provide a convoy for the beleaguered Merchant Marine fleet, who at this point had given more than anyone could have expected to the war effort. Maybe they had not signed up for combat, but it was the most combative operation of the war, and the toll on lives from all countries who signed up to provide the necessary materials of support was heavy. These new convoy vessels were a rag-tag compilation made up of former trawlers, menhaden fishing boats, sometimes called "pokey boats", and all manners of craft, which they revamped and outfitted as patrol anti-submarine boats to ride in accompaniment to the valued Merchant Marines. They were fitted with small arms necessary to fight off the undersea devils.

In the meantime, the United States was producing sufficient numbers of destroyers, and destroyer escort types of ships, along with planes classified as short-range bombers, for patrolling the skies over the infected sea. They were aware of the habit of U-boats surfacing at various times, and although they were not detected by the tankers or their escorts, they were obvious from the air and an easy target for planes.

Those days of observing the kids on their horses were coming to a close. It was ironic that one of the German captains had recently remarked, upon taking his turn at the binoculars to watch the kids on their horses, with their 'dogs', that one of the horses was pale. This was a reference to the famous quote from the Bible which made reference to "death riding a pale horse", in the Book of Revelation, the last book of the New Testament. The Lamb of God, or Lion of Judah, (Jesus Christ) opened the first four of seven seals which summoned four beings who rode on horses of white, red, black, and pale, each one symbolizing either Conquest, War, Famine, or Death. To see "death riding a pale horse", as he observed Luke on Pegasus, a horse of cream color with a white mane. That was itself a shock, but to also observe Blake on Spirit, the red horse, which was an indication of War, and then, Ellie on Blue, a totally black horse, an obvious indication of famine, his thoughts went immediately to the times they had also experienced the need of food, also of his fear of the possibility of needing food.

This scene was a shock to the German captain, and a visual omen he could not ignore. He quickly handed back the spy glass and went to his quarters totally shaking and sick to his stomach at what he felt was to follow.

Although Germany had long turned away from Christianity, the passage about the *Four Horses of the Apocalypse* was not totally unknown to them. Hitler had gone to school in a monastery and at one time considered the priesthood. Bible passages were well known by those who were educated, as the captain was.

Adding to the entourage of boats and planes to combat the U-boats were lighter than-air blimps which wafted over the ocean undetected by the enemy in their silence and were totally armed and capable of dropping killing depth charges and bombs on an easily visible target. When the children observed those most unusual air-machines, they immediately raced back to their Grandfather for an explanation. The strange craft were the talk of the school, now winding down for summer vacation. The kids of the villages were fascinated at the sight of them. Although they seldom caught one in action, they could only imagine, and scoured the sky for them and marveled as they floated over.

When school let out for the summer, the family gaily celebrated Nett's birthday. By June, the violent torpedo blasts were becoming ineffective, as only four ships were sunk, and loss of life severely cut. Grandmom made the most divine twelve-layer chocolate cake, a southern tradition. She had been saving sugar for months, even bartered for it with her friends. The gifts from the children were a topic of conversation, which required Grandmom's interpretation. Ellie gave her aunt some lace gloves but had no explanation of where they came from. Grandmom gave her a silver hand mirror, which Ellie had gotten from Aunt Rhetta's trunk. Grandmom explained that she had discovered some of the treasures given in drawers and trunks in the old house, and the kids wanted to surprise Nett. Luke gave her the loose pearls from the cave, he put them in the velvet bag Grandmom had given him, of course with Grandmom's blessings. He moved his treasures to a bag he had made for himself from some of the rawhide he got from the boot he chopped up for Ellie to carry the machete. He had learned the art from Manteo.

Blake found he could not part with his dragon, he figured his mom wouldn't appreciate it anyway; it was not her style. He gave her instead, the elephant, which actually had not been claimed. Grandpop gave her bus tickets to see her sister Iva, on the mainland. Stocky Midgett, the bus driver, organized all the connections. It seemed to be the best gift ever, if evidenced by Nett's tears. This day was the first time they had been truly happy in the new house. The war had snatched away everybody's smile.

In July, there were only ten ships stricken, but although it was a larger number, the threat was extremely restricted as Donitz pulled back his contingency of submarines and went back to the more pressing problem of the North Sea, leaving the island quiet again.

The local villagers had won, not the war, but their sanity. There were no longer burning ships, dead bodies with stiff limbs on the beach for others to find, the air was clean, but the shore was still damaged. The sea took on a sweeter smell, with only an occasional bitter reminder of what had happened to them. Tar and oil were still a problem, and lifeboats riddled with holes, remained to be burned. There were no longer funerals of those no one knew. At last, activity in the villages was more comfortable, as there ceased to be reasons to suspect that everyone without a "Hatteras brogue" was intent on killing them.

The war continued in Europe and in the Pacific; but the efforts of the talented United States workers tripped the balance toward the Allies, and slowly the enemy began to run out of supplies, added to loss of confidence with their German leaders. The citizens of Italy, the other Axis power along with Germany, murdered their leader Mussolini, and hung him, along with his mistress, upside down in the square to indicate their disapproval of the war that seemed to have no end. Great Britain succeeded in curbing the violence on the African coast.

The Japanese, stubbornly still fighting, devised a plan to send their stricken planes in a suicide dive directly into enemy ships. This act was carried out when a plane was shot out of the sky or simply out of bombs. It was called *kamikaze*. The children began to make fun of both the names of Hitler, the leader of Germany, and Mussolini, the leader of Italy, but the most fun was the name Tojo, the military leader of Japan. It was safe to say those dreaded names were soon to be no more.

Luke and Blake's dad Bill sent presents. He had become a member of the protective team which traveled with the Captain of his naval vessel, the USS *Melvile*, named for the famous writer of the book *Moby Dick*. Captain Slattery was both an Irishman, and a friend of the talents of Finnegan, also Irish, who could fix anything, and was a good man to have along. Finnegan, was also known to be good with his fists, as observed from all the boxing matches that had taken place on the ship's recreational boxing ring located on the top deck of the ship. Captain Slattery felt there was no better sailor to accompany him as he traveled on shore and took Bill along when he was on "liberty" in Europe.

Bill sent Irish lace tablecloths, mantillas, and napkins to Nett, and a rather large Irish lace tablecloth to Grandmom. To the boys he sent special Navy ribbons, and each got a set of metal toy soldiers, one set for America and one set for Germany. To Ellie he sent the most intricate collection of wooden doll furniture crafted in France that anyone could imagine. The kit was immediately assembled so the paper dolls she had cut from the Sears and Roebuck catalog, could be folded and made to sit in a chair or on the sofa. Nett then ordered a paper doll book for her, with figures that could be punched out. That took all of Ellie's time away from the boys, who could not understand the fascination, as they played "war" with each other using their new soldiers. Equally enlisting indifference from Ellie, so the three spent a few days apart. The draw of friendship eventually won over, and they were back to their old tricks again after the novelty of the new toys wore off. Blake getting them in trouble, (or himself) with the other two working to make things right.

The war overseas lasted for three more years, danger was still living in the mansion on the hill, as both Grandmom and Nett wrote long letters at night to all that were in harm's way. Uncle Wallace was in the Pacific, and had a ship shot out from under him, but he was rescued, and sent home for a while. After his recovery he was reassigned to the Loran station on the island. He was perfect as a knowledgeable wireless operator for the Navy. He later studied law at the University of North Carolina and was eventually honored as a "chair" in that department. His new assignment made Grandmom most thankful to have at least one of her sons close to home. Bill was in constant danger in Europe, and the Germans fought on, even though they began to resent the leadership of their Chancellor. At last, on May 7, 1945, Germany finally surrendered. Hitler committed suicide, and the other offending murderers were hunted. V-E Day, (victory in Europe) was celebrated on May 8, 1945. This effectively ended the war in Europe.

Nett and the three children went to New York to meet the USS Melville when Bill returned. It was a special time where they marveled at the size and look of the city of tall buildings. The elevator in their building was a sensation to the children, who had never seen such a thing. Blake was so astonished it became a problem keeping him out of it. Whenever he was missing from the hotel room, he could be found in the elevator, pushing the buttons from floor to floor. Other occupants of the hotel got used to the new "elevator man", as to their surprise, when the door opened, a little boy inquired, "floor please?" The parade down 5th Avenue, honoring the end of the war in Europe was something that was more than stirring. It was the first time the children had ever seen marching bands, and beautiful uniforms. Their hearts kept the beat with the drummers. They also had never seen so many people lining the sidewalks and did not let go of each other for the three days they were there.

The military display in the parade, delighted the boys, rows and rows of smartly marching American soldiers, doing drills and exciting everyone. There were elaborate floats and dancers from Broadway, which delighted both Nett and Ellie. Both looked at the New York ladies and their attire with shy amazement. It seemed that the store windows were also a surprising hit with the girls. It took time to drag them away. They had never seen such fancy stores inside. Ellie was most impressed when a smartly dressed smiling salesgirl stepped up to the pretty little girl and sprayed a spritz of cologne her way.

One afternoon, Bill took them to Time Square and then the Empire State building. Their eyes seemed to grow larger and larger with each bright light they saw. On top of the building there was a telescope to look out and see a view of the sprawling city. Blake was too short to look through it, so Bill lifted him, and tried to keep him from wriggling out of his arms with all his excitement. That night there was a huge display of fireworks, this was something the kids had never seen. Only a few servicemen were allowed to watch it from the top of the Empire State building as they needed special passes. The newly commissioned Admiral Slattery had gotten Bill tickets. The skyline of New York City was ablaze with colored lights forming patterns across the night canopy.

It was a vacation they would talk about forever. Nett and Bill were both holding on to the kids and each other. They even got to eat something out of an automat. A wall of windows, each displaying pieces of food on the inside. They placed their change in the slots and not really knowing if the pie or sandwich was tasty or not, it appeared they had never before eaten a decent meal. It was quite an experience. Everybody in New York was in a happy mood. There was a magical feeling throughout the city. Nobody had been as close to war as this island family, and really had no idea what the islanders had experienced. But, it was now over, and this was a great way to wipe away the awful pictures they had seen. What a special trip. They rode the train home, then went by bus to the island.

The chatter around the supper table lasted for weeks, as each remembered something they had been impressed with, and forgotten to mention before. The smiles in the old mansion were non-stop. Grandmom's boys were all coming home, Jack to the mansion, Curtis with a wife, Tommy to a government job, and Bill, the most thankful of all. He was longer in danger. His was the longest amount of time in the fighting. It took him months to calm his nerves, but the island was comforting, with the fresh breezes, the birds and cracking of the squirrels. He was not even bothered by the woodpecker which showed up. He could not stand to be alone, so the kids stayed close, they were glad he was home, and they were determined to show it. They healed him.

Meanwhile, Japan continued to fight, and seemed not to care that as a country they had lost. They refused to, according to them, "lose face", and kept on killing.

The United States took the most extreme measures ever to stop the Japanese. They chose two popular cities of Japan, Hiroshima, and Nagasaki, as representatives of what would come if they did not surrender, and dropped a bomb of tremendous power, the Atomic Bomb, on both, effectively leveling those cities, and proving what would happen if they continued in the war. The bomb wiped out 90% of Hiroshima on August 6, 1945, then when there was no official signal from the Empire of Japan of surrender, on August 8, 1945, the United States dropped a second on

Nagasaki. Finally, on August 15, the Emperor of Japan, Emperor Hirohito announced the country's unconditional surrender in a radio broadcast. The formal agreement was signed on September 2, 1945, aboard the battleship *Missouri*, anchored in Tokyo Bay. For the Japanese, it was the first siting of their exalted Emperor. V-J Day was declared on August 8, 1945.

All the boys came home for at least a rest. Some went back to the service to finish their obligations and some had completed their time. It was just the way of things, and nobody complained.

✦ 12 ✦

The Day the Dolphin Surfed

"To strive, to seek, to find, and not to yield."
Ulysses, ALFRED LORD TENNYSON

After the war left the island and moved overseas, things calmed down on the surface, but not in the souls of the islanders. There would be no peace until everyone was accounted for. Some lived, some came home injured, some returned with the war still in their spirit, and some had died.

The villagers took up where they left off, when a neighbor was sick, they sat with them, when someone died, they cooked something home-made and took it to the family, to feed both them and anyone else who came to their home to mourn. The men did not spend much time in the house, and there were still revival camp meetings in the summer. They again put up wooden swings in the yard on a strong limb of the mighty live oak trees that were prevalent on the island.

The Cardinal, the state bird, showed its beauty in the yard to remind the observer that a lost loved one, a male, was still with them, or a Blue-bird, indicating a female, was watching over and taking care. Sometimes the cardinals were so numerous that the tree looked to be burning. Men sat around new gas stoves and swapped stories. In August, "dog days" still plagued the island with mosquitoes, green flies and the stillness of no breeze. Mullet also began schooling up near the end of August, to prepare for their migration south, should they be lucky enough not to end up on a platter for supper.

Women boiled bayberry leaves until the waxy covering melted off and floated to the top. They then skimmed it off and put the wax in candle molds with a wick, for winter aromas. Baskets were made from the large blades of cattails which had bloomed in July. One could hear the cooing of doves in early morning, and the lonely hooting of a loon in the evening. A hard blow was welcomed if it was accompanied by rain to wet down the sandy soil. Communities once again gathered for "fish fry's," as the village picnic once again brought happy times.

Storms still pursued the islands following the path of the Gulf Stream in late summer and early fall, however, there was enough notice by those who followed the weather for everyone to prepare, some boring holes in the floors for incoming water to flow out, and leaving windows cracked to allow the wind to blow through. The Graveyard of the Atlantic remained a nuisance off the coast of the point in Buxton, (once called the Cape) but now mariners were aware. Still, Diamond Shoals did not cough up what she decided to keep but did continue to cast off to the natives what she did not want. There remained to be a healthy rivalry among the villages, including the Coast Guard, (now with a few Navy men left over) as shown by the summer baseball games.

Islanders were married to the sea by proximity, they studied it, respected it, fished it, used its bounty, rode on it and dreamed by it. They watched the stars from it, did not spoil it, nor did they soil it. They also did not live on it. Theirs was the back side of the island, near the sound. They set their nets in the waters off their homes, put bird blinds and hunting shacks on it, and in early morning of duck season, people could hear the crack of the shotguns, as geese and ducks were brought down for the supper tables of the villagers. They put out crab pots in the sound, for catching "a mess of hard crabs". At the end of May they walked the shore grass along the banks of the sound looking for the shedding soft crabs. Food was plentiful, and it was safe to gather it. They once again seeded their oyster and clam beds and provided the best for each other.

The villagers studied the moon and its effect on the ocean. They farmed the shore for salt from the receding tides which left a covering of the mineral in its wake. There were always bird eggs on the beach, also turtle eggs. The islanders were not in the habit of collecting either, as their chicken yards were bountiful, but the seagulls, reptiles, pelicans and ghost crabs raided the nests at will. The kids were aware of the nesting seasons, and when there were hatchlings expected, they did their best to ward off the predators, but they lost more than they saved. Only one in a hundred survived, it was a futile effort. But, nature feeds its own.

The sea also had a memory, as inlets were formed in storms, then when the islanders either built a bridge to cross them, or filled them in, years later, sometimes decades, the sea returned to the same spot and just to prove a point, it opened the same inlet again.

Hurican, the Spanish word for God or evil, brought with them ghosts of mariners, which walked the mists of the gale. They appeared as the first winds of the storm touched the island whenever the Hurricane was near. Islanders could see the storm coming in the sea and sky, blue/black, with a bright orange sunset, the dark clouds in the distance held up by sheets of rain resembling a curtain connecting the clouds and the sea, appearing to be grey walls holding up the sky. Some old timers vowed that the sound was swollen. The hurricane sent up a distinctive fresh smell, and the clouds left the sky clear as they gathered together far away, ready to come back in mass and give their strongest face to the land. When the clouds left, the sea became calm, like a mirror. When this happened, the islanders called it "the calm before a storm", and in the summer, dead calm days were suspect of harsher weather to come. The wind, on its return, revealed the cries of lost souls who perished near the shore they had once failed to attain; and ghosts of those still trapped at sea rose up in the mists to finally gain ground they could no longer touch. Some called them *gray men*, as they strode the beaches during a storm.

The sea is the closest neighbor to the island and at over three billion years old, it is guided by the waxing and waning of the stages of the moon. Waxing (increasing) for the full moon, waning (decreasing) for a new moon. Both waxing and waning look like a smile. Waxing, brightest to the left, and waning brightest to the right. The waning moon decreases in size going from a full moon to a new moon. Islanders and Indians knew this was the time to use spells that banish, or release, or reverse something. Also a time to break bad habits or bad addictions, or to end bad relationships, also a time of deep intuition. This period lasts about fourteen days in each month.

The islanders had also learned to live by the moon, as it was a time for reflection, for change if something needed reforming. They knew to plant only when the moon was "growing", never on the change, and to never cut wood on the dark of the moon, as it burned poorly. Even animals knew to breed according to the moon. After this past concentration on evil, islanders discussed getting back to nature, and began to look to the moon, stars and sea for inspiration, now that the island was rid of the evil riders. Those who went to the sea had experienced an uncomfortable reaction to the war blowing up the sea and its creatures, the same reaction they would have had at the hurting of a child. The relief that came after the war was also the return of love and appreciation of their sea. Fishermen were free to take their boats out. The sea was their neighbor, and neighbors take care of neighbors. It was a different kind of life, living by the sea, and that life was back!

The sea is 139.7 million square miles and covers 70% of the Earth's surface, and has a volume of approximately 320.3, million cubic miles. There are seven seas and five oceans. We know less about the sea than we know about the moon. There are 10,000 guiding lights who lovingly tend the sea. The Milky Way, containing 200-400 billion stars, is one of those light sources. The Milky Way is visible most nights over this island, as there is little or no ambient light here (manmade light from the land, street lights etc.). The Milky Way has at least one planet per star. There are also seventeen billion earth-sized exoplanets in the Milky Way.

The ocean stores heat and carries it to land. During the day, when the beach is hot and the water cool, the warm air from the land rises, creating a pull of cool dense air from the water over the land. The cool incoming breeze is called a sea breeze. On the island, at night, the ground loses heat quickly, while the ocean, which had been storing heat all day continues to heat the air above it, this causes a pull of cooler air away from the beach. This breeze is called a land breeze.

When the children returned home from the big city back to the island with all of its magical power, and the ocean breezes that sometimes stung their noses, back to the water that near them was so shallow, and in looking far away was so massive, they were comfortable. They rode their horses on the beach, glad there were not rows and rows of cars; beautiful as they were, this was home. There was no long metal train that rumbled over tracks, with land whizzing by; here and there was sand, some still stained, but it was their sand.

As they daily rode the beach, they were startled by the squealing of the dolphin, jumping and trying to get their attention by riding in schools with them as they traveled down the beach. Ellie was the first to dismount, and leading Blue, waded into the water to meet the excited dolphin. She longed to see Iris, with her iridescent colors sparkling through the clear ocean. Ellie was hoping that Iris would use her sonar to find her. Then, she wondered if her beautiful friend had even survived the war. After all, she was young. Ellie picked up a beautifully gossamer shell, and looked through it, seeing the rainbow of colors on the ocean. She was sad, this was only a wish. Iris was not there. She watched as the tide washed in and back out and starred at the coquina clams who rode in with the wave and stayed to bury themselves in the sand as soon as the wash meandered back to the ocean, to form a new wave and come back in and repeat the process. Realizing she had tarried too long, she turned around and looked down the beach for her cousins. She did not have to look far, they actually had never left her; they knew she was looking for Iris, and they were also searching the water for Willi and James, but the dolphins were not around.

That evening, they spent their time catching fireflies and putting them in a jar, with a lid full of tiny holes to give them air. They saw a little frog eat one, and as he walked around, for a short while his tiny belly would light up periodically. He must have swallowed it whole, and it was still glowing in his tummy. They laughed and fell on each other as the light in the frog kept going off.

They were almost ready for school to begin again, they had certainly had an exciting summer. It was going to be quite a first day, as there would be many stories from the rest of the kids as to what they had seen.

"I think we should visit the cave one more time before we have to go back to school. If we don't we will only have a little while to explore before it gets dark, this way we could spend all day." Ellie was depressed about Iris and wanted to go back and talk to Weroansquoa.

"Good idea," both boys replied.

"I think if I don't light the torches that the crystals in the walls and ceiling will light the cave." Luke had been pondering that thought for a while, as when they were there before, he was surprised that a soft wind had extinguished his torch, and there seemed to still be light. Also, he wanted to see the small beach again. He had learned in Sunday school that Noah had lit his ark with precious stones. He couldn't think of any stone that might have had a light other than crystals, and he knew they grew in caves where there was no light. The stones of Noah had to be crystals, and he couldn't wait to test his theory.

"Look! The Milky Way!" exclaimed Ellie, looking up at the stars to get a connection. "And look there, the Big Dipper!" She was staring at the sky, and mentally tracing the stars she knew.

"You know how it got its name? I read it when I was looking in the encyclopedia for information on Poseidon. Zeus and Hera, the main ancient Greek gods, had a son, Hercules, and Hera put him to her breast to feed, and he turned away, spilling her milk all over the heavens, in tiny, tiny stars. Now everyone calls it the Milky Way." Luke named his horse after the winged horse of Poseidon, given to him by his brother Zeus. In mythology, Pegasus carried the lightning bolts for Poseidon. Pegasus was a named arm of the stars of the Milky Way. Luke was always reading mythology stories about the ancient gods and the things they did. He knew his horse was named after the horse born of the god Zeus. He had studied everything on the name Pegasus.

"Coo-oo-ol!" said Blake, as he stared up to the sky at the path of tiny stars that stretched so far, looking to be so small they connected. He too was tracing the stars of the Big Dipper and looking for the more obscure Little Dipper. "Remember when we were on the ship and Captain Johns was pointing out the stars? He said they were named after animals or objects to let the sailors read where they were by the stars when they were at sea. Like a lion, or your sign Luke, the scorpion. He also talked about the North Star, and the Southern Cross, also the great collection called Orion, because it was on the equator and had the brightest lights, and was visible from everywhere, those were the ones I remembered.

"I would help you if you wanted to study the stars. I want to. We could get a book, or maybe Grandpop has one. I love them, and we can see them clearly when we know what they are. I think we need a book with the outline of each group named. That way we know how to trace them. They are not always looking exactly like what we think, but once we see the outline, we can usually understand why they are called what they are by the sailors. Like Cap'n John pointed out the lion, but I couldn't see it until he said what it was, then I could see it." Luke was always amazed at the mind of his little brother. He thought so many thoughts, and had so many dreams, he was thinking how lucky he was to have such an entertaining character around when things got dull. He was also very conscious of protecting him.

They sat on the steps of the porch, silent, lost in the thoughts of all that had happened to them, to their father, to the animals they loved, and to everyone they loved. All the while the little frog kept lighting up, he was now on the porch post. They giggled every time they saw it. Blake sat between his brother and cousin, he always wanted to be in the middle, and Luke reached over and put his arm around his shoulders. Ellie leaned over and kissed the top of his head, which was sort of damp, and smelled of sweat and probably thinking too much. They really did love each other.

"Time to come in kids, there is a great day waiting for you tomorrow. Daddy and I are going to Hatteras with Pop to bring home some hard crabs from the dock. Want crabs tomorrow night? You can go if you want to." Nett and Bill stood together in the doorway, and they had hardly been apart since he got home. The kids were just beginning to realize just how lonely their mother had been. Imagine not having your best friend to talk to, what would they do without each other?

"Mom, we had some things we were going to do tomorrow, is it O.K. if we stay around here? You and Daddy go." Luke felt like his mom and dad should have an adventure together, and, he knew the three of them were going to go back into the cave, and this would be perfect timing, with everybody else gone.

"Sure?" Nett was kind of happy to have some time alone with her husband, he had been gone so long, and she missed him. She was also proud to take him around the docks, everybody loved 'Finnegan', and she couldn't wait for the men of Hatteras docks to crowd around and welcome him home.

"Yeh Mom, you and Daddy bring us back a surprise?" Blake was also in on the plan.

The house was full now, Grandmom would not be lonely. Uncle Jack was busy hanging around with his friends, who were also home from the war, and all the guys had decided to go to college. Of course, they would take the shrimp boat across the sound to Morehead City to meet up with other friends who had cars, they were going to visit East Carolina College, and maybe State and Carolina. They had it all planned. A boy's week. When their uncles had all began to come home, he kids had offered to share a room, so Uncle Jack could have one of theirs, but he refused. He would stay on the fourth floor with Uncle Fay, in the two rooms that Uncle Jabez had used as a bedroom and a study. The study had a perfectly fine day bed in it, so the fourth floor was divided like two rooms.

Uncle Fay, home from the Merchant Marines, was in Uncle Jabez's bedroom, with a window facing the sea, and another facing the sound. It also had a fireplace, he could keep the windows up and get a cross breeze from the two waters. There were also two windows in the study, so both boys were set. It was necessary for Uncle Fay to be comfortable. He had mentally experienced a hard time while on his ship, constantly knowing he was the target of German U-boats. Also, he was dating a childhood friend who was back from the war. Her name was Amelia, and she was on leave from the Coast Guard. She and Uncle Fay would sit on the swing with their heads together, and giggle about nothing. Life was finally pleasant for everyone on the island. Sometimes Fay and Amelia would take Ol' Tony and Big Roy to the beach and stay gone for hours and hours. The sea was a great healer.

Odessa was happier than anyone had ever seen her. She was cooking so much the house smelled sweet all the time, as it gave the ocean breezes a run for their money. She would sit in the rocking chair and snap beans, humming the whole time. Or, she was picking the figs of August and canning them for Uncle Fay's favorite breakfast, figs, sharp cheese from the huge wheel on the porch, and homemade biscuits topped with Twinkle's fresh sour cream. He could not get enough. The shelves of the side porch off the kitchen were almost ready to fall down with so many things that had been preserved. She canned and jarred tomatoes, blueberries, blackberries, figs, pickled cucumbers and beets, apple sauce, grape jam, strawberry jam, and as Grandmom would say 'what-not'. It was the 'what-not' that the children liked the most. Whatever it was, it was the best. Grandmom wouldn't tell them, because it was so healthy she was afraid if they knew that, they wouldn't eat it.

Uncle Fay had brought a case of small jars of hard candy home from the ship, and since sugar was no longer rationed, there were lots of desserts which Grandpop loved. War was over, the good times were ahead. Pop stayed in his study writing letters to the government in Washington in a plea for consolidated schools, paved roads, electricity, and a plant for fresh water. He was always going somewhere to meet with other men of the villages to petition the state and federal government to obtain amenities for the island. They had earned the right to have what everybody else had, they had put their lives on the line for the country. Still, their activities and trials were not made public, time needed to pass before anyone should know of the danger that had been staved off by these brave man and women.

The following day, everybody was out early, and the kids took what they needed and went for another exploration of the caves. They waited till Uncle Fay had left so they could access the cave through the fireplace in his room. They gathered up all the things they needed that had not been left in the cave, and sneaked down the halls and steps to the cave. Immediately, they began to move through the waterfall, and the parts of the cave they were familiar with. Here they repeated the process with the torch to get rid of all unwanted insects, and it was just as pretty as before. They wanted to search for more drawings, but they were on a mission this time, so they passed up stopping to examine several rooms they had not yet explored. They made their way to the part of the cave where the roots of the trees above formed doors to secret passageways.

Ellie was the first to notice the strange smell that tickled her nose, and as slight breeze went by, she could smell the familiar aroma of Weroans-quoa. It made her smile. The cave took on a misty look, and the kids, for a minute, considered it a fog, then, they realized, it was just smoky without the smell of smoke, the air was sort of obscure. It was beginning to be damp and the roots took on a glistening from the moisture. Still, they did not associate the mist with ghosts. The moisture coming from the roots formed a glassy crystal lace across the walls. They could hear the water again as they were near the pearlescent pool, while the water that made the tiny streams ran down the middle of the dead leaves that covered the floor of the cave. The wolves were right beside them, accompanied by their pups, which were growing so much they were almost as tall as their elders, but they were so skinny, and so rambunctious that it was obvious they were young.

Then, Blake felt the breeze, and of course he said something.

"Boy, where is the wind coming from?" he said in a whisper to Luke. He sounded a little worried, like maybe there was going to be a cave-in.

"Look," Luke pointed to the ceiling, clearly seen with mist having disappeared, the blue and silver light was shining on the ceiling, just like the magic book had lit the secret room of the third floor. But this time there were friendly apparitions and three shadowy spirits floating above their heads. Once again, the torch located in a crevice on the far wall went out as if it was blown out. Just as he suspected, the crystals embedded in the walls and ceiling provided enough light for them to see. Twylah sat down right beside Ellie, and with her head lowered and ears forward, she rested her big head next to Ellie, in a gesture of respect. The three shamans watched in their mist, now clearly detected by the light of the crystals.

Blake put out his hand to touch Mingin, but his hand went through the shadow like it was only smoke. He drew back quickly.

"Don't worry Blake, he's only a memory, and he's here because you were his best friend. Remember how he said you were the only one who ever visited him? You didn't know he was so special and powerful, but he came with Powwaw and Weroansquoa, and they came with the knowledge of the holy ones from before, when they were forced to leave Poseidon's palace as it sank under the sea. The three of them came carrying the wolves, for protection, just like us, and they found this island. We are seeing the history of our island." Ellie spoke like a much older person now, she seemed to have confidence and knowledge. She had just communicated with Twylah, though the boys did not know it.

Luke put his hand in the luminous pool, and again it formed an irregular stone of colorful beauty. He pressed it into Blake's hand.

"I think it's good luck," he said. "Keep it just in case."

Their hair was slightly blowing as the apparitions moved around. They kept circling the children, sort of like protection. The shaman knew that Suki was in the area, they could tell by the way Rafe was barring his teeth when he looked in a particular direction.

Luke dipped his hand in the pool again, this time giving another colorful stone to Ellie.

"Put this in your dress pocket, something inside tells me it is protection. I feel it strongly, so, I want to make sure I pay attention. It is Powwaw talking to me. I feel like I could stay here forever. Does everyone feel the same things I am feeling? I feel strong."

"Me too," said Blake.

Ellie closed her eyes and reached out her hands to the boys. As the water from above dripped like pearls down the tree roots, they widened, revealing beyond the white sandy beach framed by the leaves of the trees and the bushes; it looked like a beach in a picture frame. Beyond, was a calm blue ocean with soft waves washing into the shore. The wolves went first, the blue and silver light fading from over their heads as they exited the cave and walked through the opening. The pups ran past them to the ocean for a swim, as Rafe, Theo and Twylah turned around to watch the kids come through the frame. When they stepped on the pure, white, fine sand, the roots again closed the portal and the kids saw the three wolves face them and drop prone in front of them, paws out, heads down and looking up in reverence for the children they were privileged to protect. The pups, sensing something special was happening, bounded out of their play in the ocean and dropped down beside their elders trying to emulate their position as with their heads down and their eyes looking up as if to say, "is this right?"

As the kids stepped out of the opening, they did not notice what the wolves had seen. Before them, beyond the breakers were two great blue horses, with their bodies more out of the ocean than they had ever seen them; as they pawed at the breakers, they had fish tails. The kids had discussed that books said Poseidon was pulled by seahorses, but when they read about them in the encyclopedia, seahorses were only inches long. These were huge, and now they realized they were Sea Horses. Horses of the sea, with tails for back legs. It reminded them of the mermen, whose bodies resembled a man, but they had the skin and tails of a dolphin, from having morphed over time to adapt from land to sea. These horses belonged to Poseidon, and, when he was at sea, his body also took on the appearance of a sea creature, and he had the lower body of a dolphin. The adaptation for their environment was something the kids had never thought of.

Luke starred at the massive creatures in the ocean in front of him. He caught the crystal that Poseidon tossed to him, and displayed a wide grin as he heard the sea god let out that thunderous laugh. With an equally wide smile, and probably a laugh, he put the silver thread with the beautiful crystal around him, and as he walked into the ocean, the sargassum mats floated forward, and he began to be wrapped in the silver suit being fashioned by the thread around his neck. Willi waited.

Ellie and Blake were experiencing the same thing, they were breathless, excited, surprised and wondering if their dolphin had survived, or would they be greeted by other friends. Ellie laughed out loud as she reached out for her sargassum matt and from the corner of her eye, she saw the glistening colors of Iris. The thread weaved itself into a suit and mask of seaworthy protection, and as she climbed on the mat, Iris ducked below to come up under it, while the thread, still weaving, created a saddle for her to ride.

Blake hardly waited for his suit to be formed, he was so anxious to be connected to James, the youngest of the group, both dolphin and rider almost ducked under the water too soon, and Poseidon put out his hand to hold them above, until the suit was ready to protect them. It was the first time the children had ever heard the roaring laugh of the mighty leader from the sea. It was so hearty, it seemed to call down the heavens.

The familiar rush of the ocean was now surrounding them. The dolphin headed to the Hatteras slough, between the shoals. Here there was no evidence of war. Only the flora and fauna of a crystal sea. The water was clear and beautiful, they could see the bottom, as conchs scoured for food, and loose clams and scallops rolled around in the pull of the tide. Familiar fish swam by, seeming to greet them, sea grass with tiny Seahorses clinging to the stalks, swayed as they passed. Shards of sunlight pierced the water creating multiple colors of green and yellow. Closer to the floor of the ocean were clumps of coral in shades of pink and orange, they saw a starfish curled up in the broken half of a clam.

Continuing on beneath the calm sea, Harvest fish seemed entangled in a Sea Nettle, and shone like the crystals around their neck, through the lacy translucent fingers the nettle sent out. The cap of it, as it opened and closed to move forward, seemed to carry the little fish around the children and their dolphin.

The dolphin were trying to cleanse the souls of the children they were carrying. On the bottom they saw gray and silver Sea Anemone attached to a sponge. A Cobia was catching a draft from the back of a huge Stingray, who also had a tiny parasite rider which was stuck between his eyes. It was amazing to see along the rocky bottom the beautiful yellow and gray Spotfin Butterflyfish, whose prominent yellow fin was in total contrast to the broken shells and growing coral clumps. Next to them was the ornate Diamond Back Terrapin Turtle, with his perfectly correct squares of shell casing catching their eye. Could he have also been born on the beaches of Hatteras?

The dolphin began to rise from their art aquarium and in the climb they came close to a large Loggerhead attempting to keep up with them. Maybe he was one of the babies they had saved from the seagulls' years before. The funniest fish they saw were the blue Lookdowns, whose heads were shaped in a way that made their eyes always looking down. When Luke turned around and pointed them out to the others, it made them laugh.

Breaking the plane of the water, they were on a wave that was cresting, and the children realized they were about to surf in close to the shore on the back of a dolphin.

The dolphins raced down the face of the wave beside each other, and just as they thought they would reach the beach, each dolphin turned left and went under the barrel of the huge wave. It was like being in a water tunnel, and there seemed to be no end. Just before the wave planed out, the dolphin turned left again, this time heading out to sea. Today the ocean was calm, and the sun danced across the top in such an even line, that it appeared to be a highway ahead of them. It even seemed that the stars had fallen on the top of the ocean, as sparkles appeared on and beside the new path toward the horizon. The sun was also sparkling off the crystal suits of the children and attracting other dolphins. Soon there was a school, jumping and diving around the silver suited children, and their own dolphin were also diving and jumping along with their friends. All three kids were holding on for dear life, but the crystal threads holding them to the sargassum mats was strong, and the riders were perfectly safe.

The playful dolphins edged closer and closer to the area of shoals called The Diamonds, where many ships were previously lost and the site of new wrecks from the recent activity from the German U-boats. The dolphins were taking them to see the destruction inflicted on their area of the ocean. As they neared the dreaded shoals, the dolphin, all of them, the ones carrying the children, and the ones who had shown up to play, all dove down for a look. Here on the ocean were some of the ships who had found their final resting place. Already the wrecks were teaming with all types of fish, some in schools, following one after another, or bunched up, but, the ships were not alone. The final resting

*place for those destroyed in the war were accompanied by the creatures of the
sea. The friendly creatures of the sea. It was a new community.*

*Upon seeing the blue ocean blanket that wrapped the unfortunate victims
of such horror, the silence of it all was not lost on the three riders. They too
moved in and around the metal structures that now occupied the deep and
saw the life that had also decided to live around it. The ships rested quietly.*

*The school of dolphin began to swim toward the sun, and soon shards of
light penetrated the solid blue curtains as they rippled with different hues of the
deep blue sea. The water began to turn from blue to green as the light mingled
with the deep, and soon the company surfaced, and began to make their way
once more toward the shore. The children soon could see the outline of their
beloved lighthouse in the distance and felt a warm familiarity of comfort which
it had always provided.*

*As they neared the shore, all but three of the dolphins veered away, and
Willi, James and Iris, carrying their special friends, moved ahead once again
to the shore, and to the rise and fall of the waves which would eventually touch
the beaches of Cape Hatteras. As the dolphins moved close, the waves carried
them close enough for the children to touch, and one by one they dismounted,
and with a lighter heart, and an assurance that the ocean was once again
their friend, they dismounted, and half swam, half walked through the shore
breakers to the sandy beach of the Lighthouse. Waiting for them in the dunes
were Pegasus, Blue and Spirit, miraculously walking among the sea oats of the
dunes, appearing to graze as they waited for their masters.*

The children sat on the beach for a while, in total silence. Each was
thinking of what they had seen and what it meant to them. They were
comfortable where they were, and had familiar strength around them,
in the lighthouse and their trusted friends, the horses. As they sat, they
became aware that their wolves had joined them, not sitting, but stretched
out on the sand, as if to be sunning themselves. It was autumn, and the
breeze from the ocean was fresh and warm. For the moment, the smell
of tar and oil was not there. They stared out to sea and saw that their

dolphin had joined their school of friends and were also comfortable enough to put on a tail walking, tandem jumping show for them. Some even surfed the large breakers off shore.

The sky was streaked with blue and silver through the cloud formations that formed first one shape, then another. Luke began to pick out shapes he recognized, a raven, head of a wolf: Ellie, an old man, maybe Poseidon, a trident: Blake, saw a frog wearing a hat, and a bit of a castle. They were lost in the clouds, each changing to something even more outrageous, and they began to laugh. Finally, they realized they were hungry, and with light hearts, they raced to their horses and headed home.

Of course, Grandmom was waiting with an understanding smile, and a plate of cookies. Pop, on the other hand was in his study, working on some project that would further the advancement of the island. There was his constant petitions for all the schools to be consolidated into one community. That meant paved roads between the villages. He was in contact with the Rural Electrical Association of the U.S. Government for wires to be strung giving electricity to all the homes and businesses of the island. His rushing out to the Coast Guard Station was switched to going in the evening to one of the school houses, or grocery stores in the various villages to meet with other men who wanted the same thing he did. The communities began to work for progress. Sometimes they went to community meetings in Manteo, to meet with people of the county, to push for better representation for the island. Grandpop was voted on to be County Commissioner representing the island as a part of deciding what the best way was to stay connected. There was no turning back, the island was an active part of the government, and the men began to meet with off islanders to better provide for services for the seven villages. The work continued, other men were also voted to positions of authority to handle various areas of concern.

All of the wishes of Cape Hatteras Island were met. Over the years, roads were built, electricity and city water was provided, schools were consolidated, men were put on county councils to voice the wishes of the island, and they were heard and respected. Many men eventually represented the island in various projects, all for the good of the seven villages. And, the island changed, and, in becoming more modern, more island children attended college, and changed the island again.

It was a wonderful time to have lived here when it was "just us", but all things change.

What did not change in all of that was the adventurous spirit of the three Jennette children, the mysteries of the huge stone house, and the secrets of the network of hidden caves.

Life had truly returned to normal, if one would call this normal.

Interesting Facts about the Island

Many have looked to this area when searching to be "off the grid." The island is friendly enough to accept strangers, and to help with their ambitions, especially if the aim is to enhance what is already here. This final epilogue discusses some of these men, and their need to accomplish a goal.

Islanders have both been slow to recognize the need to protect the land, and to distinguish who, among strangers, had ill intentions at their expense. The most glaring misuse by locals was the theory that being surrounded by water, there was no need to fence in their domestic animals. Thus, as these very animals were allowed to roam free, without fear of their wandering off, they fed on the tender shoots of vegetation and trees that would have naturally produced rebirth of destruction from the yearly hurricanes and storms that prevailed upon this strip of land every year. Ignorance of what would happen to future growth, was a horrible oversight.

Islanders always had what they needed to subsist. They were isolated from the mainland and did not anticipate overpopulation. What they had seemed to be enough. Thus, rebirth of the natural woodland was stunted by lack of foresight. This also prevented them from recognizing the same quality in strangers who denuded the plentiful forests of the

island in exchange for promised wealth. Wealth of both the perpetra-
tor, and the recipient. Time has proven the mistakes of the past, and as
a people, advantage has been taken of many resources in exchange for
greed. In this case, it was nature that suffered. Soon, the seas will suffer
the same plight, as overfishing, pollution and man, attempt to use up
what is available, never considering it will soon disappear.

Not all strangers who came to these shores, simply took what they
wanted and left. There have been those who used the island and its
people, and with respect for what they observed, gave back. Included
in these facts, omitted from the narrative, are names of those men who
did not take advantage, but observed what was here, and attempted to
enhance the wealth of resources with a more modern approach to make
life easier for their hosts. These men simply saw a need of kind people
and shared their knowledge to advance the lives and comfort of the hos-
pitable natives.

On this island, the Indians who first inhabited the land, were never
thrown off, nor removed to make way for a more modern society. The
Indians eventually disappeared from this land by diseases unfamiliar to
their culture and brought in by the strangers they welcomed. By 1750,
most were replaced by their offspring, who were a mixed breed of both
European and Native American.

And, yes, there were slaves on the island. Their treatment was not
chronicled. However. we know that when the Union Army invaded the
island, some fled to the mainland, and total freedom, while others stayed,
and as free men, enjoyed the same plight as the natives. In times of prosperity, they prospered, in times of want, they also shared that.

Most strangers were aware of the island through its bountiful supply
of fowl and fish. The sport of hunting has historically fascinated humans.
Of course, the islanders hunted for sustenance, but the supply was so
plentiful of everything that flew or swam, that others were able to enjoy
the abundance for sport. The following men were introduced to this

area through their love of sport. Once here and taken with the skills and camaraderie of their guides, they did attempt to share their talents and wealth in an attempt to give back.

One such man was Thomas Spurgeon Eaton, the son of Reynolds Tobacco. As a friend of Hatterasman Frasier Peele, a fisherman, he financed and built an ice plant in the sound off the coast of Hatteras Village for commercial fishermen to store their fish and keep it fresh until ready for market. Formerly, the only way to preserve the catch was to salt it down. This restricted the type of fish that could be transported. The fish had to be oily, like menhaden or spot. This was a small sample of the wealth of fish available to transport. So, Eaton, stepped in and provided the island fishermen with a more realistic opportunity for commerce. He financed an ice plant, built on stilts in the Pamlico Sound, and provided electricity necessary to sustain the ice. He was also responsible for electricity to the whole of the village of Hatteras. Eaton shared his wealth of knowledge with newspaper men from the northern states, and Hatteras became a considered supply market for those in need of freshly caught fish. He not only provided the necessary tools to become successful in making a living in commercial fishing, but indirectly introduced the possibility of off shore sport-fishing to those who fished for large trophy fish caught off the island, as he was one of the first to fish the Gulf Stream.

Hatteras became a destination for fishermen, and as a result catered to them with motels and restaurants, resulting in an enhanced economy for the locals. It was not long for this new opportunity to pique the interest of other innovative local men. Ernal Foster, and his brother Bill, commissioned the building of a proper sea going boat. Designed and built by Calvin and Corky Burrus, the *Jackie Fay*, opened up a new possibility for a new livelihood for fishermen. As a result of off shore sport fishing expeditions, the island became known as the Blue Marlin Capitol of the World. Soon men built clubhouses to entertain the fishermen and their wives as they enjoyed all day trips to the Gulf Stream for fishing the large catches of blue and white marlin and sailfish among other the trophy catches. Local captains either used their own vessels or signed on to pilot the large yachts belonging to wealthy men who were not familiar with these waters.

The introduction of sport fishing led to Hunt Clubs constructed by those who visited for the sport of hunting ducks and geese, also in abundance, when they desired more than the local comfort of a sink blind. These men gathered together and built Club houses on stilts in the Pamlico Sound, for the purpose of staying overnight, or several days, in comfort. Of course, these clubs hired local men to guide them in the art of bringing down multiples of fowl, and in the 1930's this also provided a livelihood for local men.

The island was not a well-kept secret, as the wealth of natural resources brought many to its shores to partake. General Billy Mitchell met and befriended Alaska Jennette, a native of Buxton, and was captivated by his stories of the abundance of geese and ducks to native to the area and found in the waters off the island. He traveled with Jennette to the island to participate in his hobby of hunting fowl. Mitchell found a home among the men of like-minded relaxation, and he stayed for weeks at a time, during his R&R from military duty, hunting during the daytime, using clubs available, and playing cards with the locals at night. All the local men knew Mr. Billy. It was eventually here he proved his theory that planes could be used in warfare as he flew his personal plane, a De Havilland model, to the solid beach off Hatteras village. There, he orchestrated an attack on two warships anchored off the Carolina coast, sinking both, to prove his point.

Using locals to introduce off islanders to the secrets of this island was the same theory as those in earlier years needing to traverse the sound without running into the shifting shoals that plagued those unfamiliar with the area. The strangers hired local captains from both Ocracoke and Hatteras villages to pilot them through, the unfamiliar waters with shifting shoals built up by wind and weather and unseen by novices. This gave access to cities of mainland North Carolina for trade and eventually for war. Piloting became a lucrative business.

The island has been visited by at least two Presidents, Herbert Hoover, who came after viewing Kitty Hawk, where the Wright Brothers flew the first plane, and Harry Truman, who came to fish the waters of the Gulf Stream. Other noted fishermen were Andy Griffin, the famous actor, who discovered the island when he appeared in the outdoor drama, *The Lost Colony*, playing Sir Walter Raleigh. Charles Lindberg, in 1927, forced to stay overnight on the island of Ocracoke, and said of the cook at the Coast Guard station there, that it was the best beans he had ever tasted. As a gesture of his thanks, he offered the cook an opportunity to accompany him in a short flight in his plane, *Spirit of St. Louis*, but the cook told him he was "just fine on the ground." There is no record of whether the cook regretted his decision. Also, Jimmy Buffett, the singer, also visited the station in Ocracoke in the year 2000, after being grounded due to inclement weather.

Alexander Hamilton had his unlucky introduction to the island when he passed within a few miles of the cape at Buxton on the ship *Thunderbolt* and experienced a fire at sea. He dubbed the area known as Diamond Shoals, *The Graveyard of the Atlantic*, and when he was first in Congress, recommended establishing a lighthouse on Hatteras Island. The experience forever changed him, as he later worked with both the lighthouse services and the Coast Guard. The locals always referred to the Cape Hatteras lighthouse as "Mr. Hamilton's light."

In 1768. Benjamin Franklin, while in England, became interested in ocean currents, and the time it took for ships to navigate certain waters. There seemed to be a current that delivered ships faster than the surrounding ocean. After studying whale behavior, water temperatures and change in color, Franklin discovered that this river within the ocean, dwarfed all other rivers which emptied into the Atlantic combined. The proximity of the fast moving river" also contributed to the path of storms, and coastal erosion the closer the land was to the stream, later named the Gulf Stream. The proximity of the Gulf Stream runs closest to Cape Hatteras Island than any other land mass of the United States, and provides a path for hurricanes to follow, as its warm water encourages both the wind and temperatures of a storm to follow its path.

The Gulf Stream is sixty-two miles wide, and 3,900 feet deep. The area is so deep, the water is a different color from its surround. One can tell the entrance into the Gulf Stream by the deep blue color of the water, in contrast to the greenish color of the ocean it touches. The closeness of the current steals fourteen feet of beach each year and moves the island 50-200 feet west each century.

The island existed through the fifties without a fire station, the bucket brigade and hand pumps were the only defense from fire. As a result, island houses usually had a detached kitchen, knowing the majority of fires originated from the kitchen. There was hardly a family in the old days that did not have to deal with a fire. Along with no fire department, there was also no police department. Men took care of culprits in an island fashion, which did not entail incarceration. Because of the problem one faced in leaving the island, few practiced their life of crime here. Those bent on crime, took it off the island.

Probably the most famous visitors were those who found the island air and sea currents most conducive to their inventions dealing with the travel of sound. Those men included Aubrey Fessenden, who was responsible for sonar; and Guglielrmo Marconi, the telegraph key, radio transmission, transatlantic telegraph cables, and transmission of voice through radio broadcast were most familiar to islanders. Both Fessenden and Marconi fought over patents until their death, and both erected tall radio towers in what is now Frisco village, for their experiments. Lee de Forest, also visited the island for his experiments, and eventually was credited with the development of sound-on-film, used for the motion pictures, as well as a tube which enabled weak signals to be amplified and transmitted over longer distances. All studied at one time under Thomas Edison.

The talented locals were responsible for two rather unusual structures. The first at Beacon Island, a hill in the Pamlico Sound in the inlet between Portsmouth Island and Ocracoke, built on a particularly tall collection of oyster shells. The man-made island measured almost twenty acres and was used as a trading post. During the Civil War, it was the site of a Confederate Army Post, and eventually destroyed by the Union Navy. It was reduced to seven and one half acres and is now a bird sanctuary. It was used by the Pirates in the 1700s to off-load booty in anticipation of moving it further inland.

Shell Castle Island was another natural island built on sand, rock and shells, close to Ocracoke Island. It housed buildings for trade, and one of North Carolina's first lighthouses with a shingle exterior. It was a "lightering post", used to off load materials from a large boat, not suitable for traversing the shallow sound, to a smaller vessel or barge with a shallower draft, capable of maneuvering shoals in the sound. The structure was built on old oyster beds and was about one half mile long and sixty feet long. The shells were more resistant to waves and wind and was situated near a deep passage. It also boasted a windmill, a gristmill, a store, lumber yard, notary public, tavern and a building about three hundred feet long used for storage filled with supplies necessary for ships. It was destroyed in 1806 by a hurricane, thus adding another shoal, hindering access to the sound. This unsuspecting obstacle prevented those without knowledge from entering the channel to gain access to the inland cities.

The history of Cape Hatteras partially included the now island of Ocracoke, which until 1848 was connected as one, when a hurricane separated the two, its rich in history beyond what is now available to observe. In reading these five books, the original look, and the early activities that made up what is now a tourist destination should be interesting to those who visit, have, or anticipate having a home here. These oddities are what make people treasure the island and admire the local inhabitants. It is more than mac-mansions, and sandy beaches. The natives have struggled and fought to preserve what is here. They went through the hard years, only to see what you see now. Try to realize there were no locals living on the beach side of the island. What you see in all the homes lining the oceanfront are strangers. They came to enjoy what the natives have built and loved for over four hundred years. Still, the new sidewalks and stoplights were built at the request of those who came here from somewhere else to live. Like those who discovered this continent, these people struggle to make this island a mirror of what they left that they did not like. It is the nature of the beast.

Welcome to this island, located at the edge of the world. Try to save what can be saved, or it will become what you left behind.

CPSIA information can be obtained
at www.ICGtesting.com
Printed in the USA
JSHW010829010819
1011JS00001B/4